Contents

Introduction

The Saxon Homeschool Testing Book for Geometry contains Tests, a Testing Schedule, Test Answer Forms, and Test Solutions. Descriptions of these components are provided below.

About the Tests

The tests are available after every five lessons, beginning after Lesson 10. The tests are designed to provide students with sufficient time to learn and practice each concept before they are assessed. The test design allows students to display the skills they have developed, and it fosters confidence that will benefit students when they encounter comprehensive standardized tests.

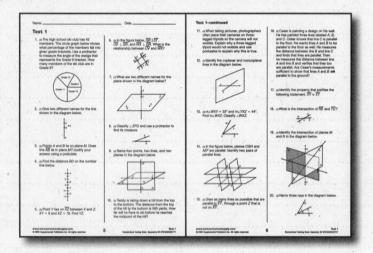 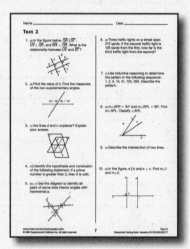

Testing Schedule

Administering the tests according to the schedule is essential. Each test is written to follow a specific five-lesson interval in the textbook. Following the schedule allows students sufficient practice on new topics before they are assessed on those topics.

Tests should be given after every fifth lesson, beginning after Lesson 10. The testing schedule is explained in greater detail on page 4 of this book.

Homeschool Testing Book: Geometry SV 9781600329777

Optional Test Solution Answer Forms are included in this book. Each form provides a structure for students to show their work.

About the Test Solution Answer Forms

This book contains three kinds of answer forms for the tests that you might find useful. These answer forms provide sufficient space for students to record their work on tests.

ANSWER FORM A: TEST SOLUTIONS

This is a double-sided master with a grid background and partitions for recording the solutions to twenty problems.

ANSWER FORM B: TEST SOLUTIONS

This is a double-sided master with a plain, white background and partitions for recording the solutions to twenty problems.

ANSWER FORM C: TEST SOLUTIONS

This is a single-sided master with partitions for recording the solutions to twenty problems and a separate answer column on the right-hand side.

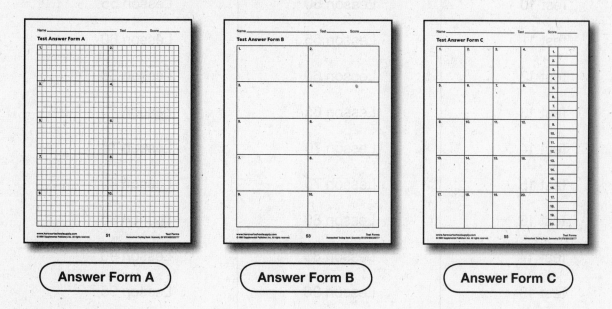

Answer Form A   Answer Form B   Answer Form C

Test Solutions

The Test Solutions are designed to be representative of students' work. Please keep in mind that problems may have more than one correct solution. We have attempted to stay as close as possible to the methods and procedures outlined in the textbook.

Testing Schedule

Test to be administered:	Covers material through:	Give after teaching:
Test 1	Lesson 5	Lesson 10
Test 2	Lesson 10	Lesson 15
Test 3	Lesson 15	Lesson 20
Test 4	Lesson 20	Lesson 25
Test 5	Lesson 25	Lesson 30
Test 6	Lesson 30	Lesson 35
Test 7	Lesson 35	Lesson 40
Test 8	Lesson 40	Lesson 45
Test 9	Lesson 45	Lesson 50
Test 10	Lesson 50	Lesson 55
Test 11	Lesson 55	Lesson 60
Test 12	Lesson 60	Lesson 65
Test 13	Lesson 65	Lesson 70
Test 14	Lesson 70	Lesson 75
Test 15	Lesson 75	Lesson 80
Test 16	Lesson 80	Lesson 85
Test 17	Lesson 85	Lesson 90
Test 18	Lesson 90	Lesson 95
Test 19	Lesson 95	Lesson 100
Test 20	Lesson 100	Lesson 105
Test 21	Lesson 105	Lesson 110
Test 22	Lesson 110	Lesson 115
Test 23	Lesson 115	Lesson 120

Homeschool Testing Book: Geometry SV 9781600329777

Test 1

1. (3) The high school ski club has 42 members. The circle graph below shows what percentage of the members fall into given grade brackets. Use a protractor to measure the angle of the wedge that represents the Grade 9 bracket. How many members of the ski club are in Grade 9?

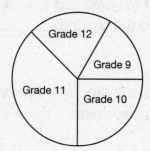

2. (1) Give two different names for the line shown in the diagram below.

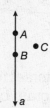

3. (4) Points A and B lie on plane M. Does line $\overleftrightarrow{AB}$ lie in plane M? Justify your answer using a postulate.

4. (2) Find the distance BD on the number line below.

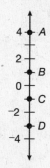

5. (2) Point Y lies on $\overline{XZ}$ between X and Z. XY = 9 and XZ = 19. Find YZ.

6. (5) In the figure below, $\overleftrightarrow{QR} \parallel \overleftrightarrow{ST}$, $\overleftrightarrow{UV} \perp \overleftrightarrow{QR}$, and $\overleftrightarrow{WX} \perp \overleftrightarrow{QR}$. What is the relationship between $\overleftrightarrow{UV}$ and $\overleftrightarrow{WX}$?

7. (1) What are two different names for the plane shown in the diagram below?

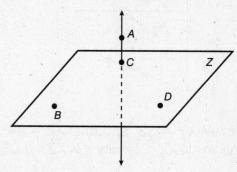

8. (3) Classify ∠EFG and use a protractor to find its measure.

9. (4) Name four points, two lines, and two planes in the diagram below.

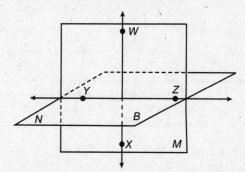

10. (2) Teddy is skiing down a hill from the top to the bottom. The distance from the top of the hill to the bottom is 565 yards. How far will he have to ski before he reaches the midpoint of the hill?

Test 1–continued

11. (4) When taking pictures, photographers often place their cameras on three-legged tripods so the camera will not wobble. Explain why a three-legged tripod would not wobble and use postulates to explain why this is true.

12. (1) Identify the coplanar and noncoplanar lines in the diagram below.

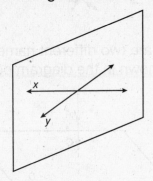

13. (3) m∠WXY = 33° and m∠YXZ = 44°. Find m∠WXZ. Classify ∠WXZ.

14. (5) In the figure below, planes CGH and AEF are parallel. Identify two pairs of parallel lines.

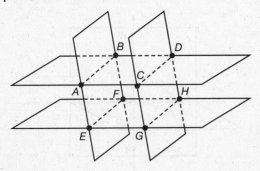

15. (5) Draw as many lines as possible that are parallel to $\overleftrightarrow{XY}$, through a point Z that is not on $\overleftrightarrow{XY}$.

16. (5) Cesar is painting a design on his wall. He has painted three lines labeled A, B, and C. Cesar knows that line C is parallel to the floor. He wants lines A and B to be parallel to the floor as well. He measures the distance between line B and line C and finds that they are parallel. Then he measures the distance between line A and line B and verifies that they too are parallel. Are Cesar's measurements sufficient to show that lines A and B are parallel to the ground?

17. (2) Identify the property that justifies the following statement. $\overline{XY} \cong \overline{XY}$

18. (1) What is the intersection of $\overrightarrow{RS}$ and $\overrightarrow{TU}$?

19. (4) Identify the intersection of planes M and N in the diagram below.

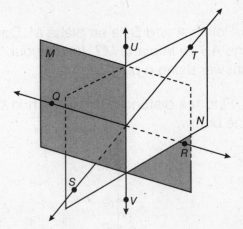

20. (3) Name three rays in the diagram below.

Homeschool Testing Book: Geometry SV 9781600329777

Test 2

1. (5) In the figure below, $\overrightarrow{QR} \parallel \overrightarrow{ST}$, $\overrightarrow{UV} \perp \overrightarrow{QR}$, and $\overrightarrow{WX} \perp \overrightarrow{QR}$. What is the relationship between $\overrightarrow{UV}$ and $\overrightarrow{ST}$?

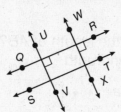

2. (6) Find the value of x. Find the measures of the two supplementary angles.

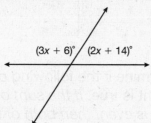

$(3x + 6)°$ $(2x + 14)°$

3. (1) Are lines d and n coplanar? Explain your answer.

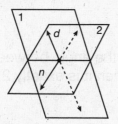

4. (10) Identify the hypothesis and conclusion of the following statement: If a prime number is greater than 2, then it is odd.

5. (Inv. 1) Use the diagram to identify all pairs of same-side interior angles with transversal a.

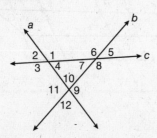

6. (2) Three traffic lights on a street span 210 yards. If the second traffic light is 125 yards from the first, how far is the third traffic light from the second?

7. (7) Use inductive reasoning to determine the pattern in the following sequence: 1, 2, 5, 14, 41, 122, 365. Describe the pattern.

8. (3) $m\angle APR = 34°$ and $m\angle RPL = 56°$. Find $m\angle APL$. Classify $\angle APL$.

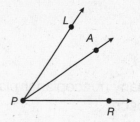

9. (4) Describe the intersection of two lines.

10. (5) In this figure, $a \parallel b$ and $a \perp c$. Find $m\angle 1$ and $m\angle 2$.

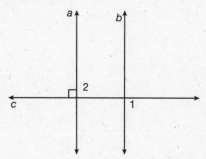

Test 2–continued

11. (8) Find the area of a right triangle with a hypotenuse of 17 m and a leg of 6 m. Round to the nearest hundredth.

12. (6) Which angle is complementary to ∠RKP? Which angle is supplementary to it?

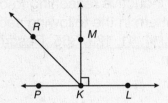

13. (7) Use inductive reasoning to determine the next term in the series: 21, 26, 23, 28, 25, 30, 27, ____.

14. (1) How many noncoplanar planes define space?

15. (2) K, L, and M are collinear points such that L is between K and M. If $LM = 8 - 3x$ and $KM = 12x + 17$, find KL in terms of x.

16. (8) If a regular triangle has a perimeter of $18x + 27$, what is an expression for the length of one of its sides?

17. (9) What is the length of $\overline{AB}$? Round to the nearest hundredth.

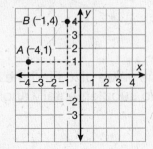

18. (10) Determine if the following conditional statement is true. *If the sum of two integers is even, then both of them are even.* If it is false, give an example that shows why it is false.

19. (3) What is the angle between the hands of a clock when it is exactly 2 o'clock?

20. (4) Among the labeled points, how many triples of collinear points are there in this figure? List these triples.

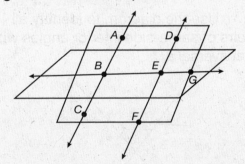

Homeschool Testing Book: Geometry SV 9781600329777

Test 3

1. (3) m∠WXY = 26° and m∠YXZ = 57°. Find m∠WXZ. Classify the angle.

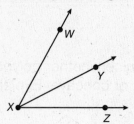

2. (6) Determine the values of x and y in the diagram.

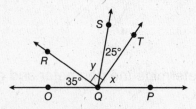

3. (1) Identify the coplanar and noncoplanar lines in the diagram below.

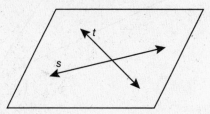

4. (14) Find a counterexample to this conjecture. If a quadrilateral has two pairs of congruent sides, it is a parallelogram.

5. (13) The base of a triangle measures 4 cm and its area is 21.4 cm². Determine the height of this triangle.

6. (12) Prove that lines a and b are parallel.

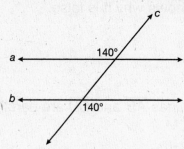

7. (7) Use inductive reasoning to determine the next term in the series: 1, 4, 10, 19, 31, 46, ____.

8. (8) Michael wants to carpet his living room floor. If the floor is a rectangle that is 16 feet by 21 feet, determine the area of the floor in square feet.

9. (12) Prove that lines m and n are parallel.

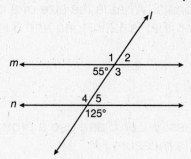

10. (9) Calculate the distance between two points A(8, ⁻6) and B(12, ⁻3).

Homeschool Testing Book: Geometry SV 9781600329777

11. *(10)* Determine whether the following conditional statement is true. *If $x^2 = 64$, then x = 8.* If it is false, give an example that shows why it is false.

12. *(Inv. 1)* Lines $\overleftrightarrow{AB}$ and $\overleftrightarrow{CD}$ are parallel. Find m∠CLM.

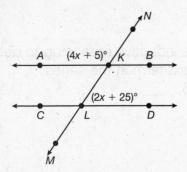

13. *(11)* Determine the midpoint of the line segment connecting (−1, 3) and (−6, −3).

14. *(8)* A rectangular computer screen is measured by the length of one of its diagonals. What is the size of a computer screen that is 12 in. long and 9 in. high?

15. *(3)* Classify ∠JKL and use a protractor to find its measure.

16. *(11)* Determine the midpoint C of the line segment $\overline{AB}$ connecting A(−3, 5.2) and B(4.6, −2.2).

17. *(15)* Determine whether polygon JKLMNO is convex or concave. Explain.

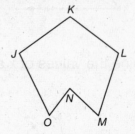

18. *(13)* Determine the perimeter and area of ∆ABC.

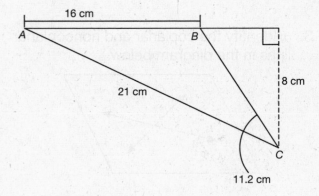

19. *(10)* State the hypothesis and the conclusion of this conjecture. *If the product of two integers is divisible by 6, then one of these numbers is divisible by 3, and the other number is divisible by 2.* Is this conjecture true? Explain how you know.

20. *(14)* Find a counterexample to this conjecture. *The sum of any two integers that are greater than 1 is less than their product.*

Test 4

1. (17) Identify the hypothesis and the conclusion in the statement below. Then, write the negation of each.

   If Lucy buys a salad, then she buys a sandwich.

2. (1) What is the intersection of $\overleftrightarrow{AB}$ and $\overleftrightarrow{MN}$ in the diagram below?

   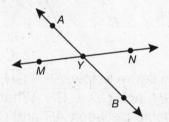

3. (Inv. 2) A right triangle has a hypotenuse of 30 inches and one leg that measures 24 inches. What is the length of the third side?

4. (6) Identify two sets of adjacent angles and one linear pair in the diagram below.

   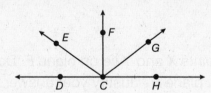

5. (9) Find the distance between the points $(^-4, 6)$ and $(^-4, ^-2)$.

6. (12) Prove that lines *a* and *b* in the diagram below are parallel.

   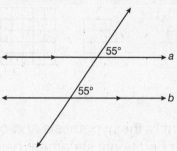

7. (15) Name the polygon below. Determine whether it is equiangular, equilateral, regular, irregular, or more than one of these.

8. (18) In the right triangle *RST*, m∠*S* = 21° and the right angle is at vertex *R*. Find the measure of ∠*T*.

9. (3) Name three rays in the diagram below.

10. (19) Determine the perimeter and area of the square below.

    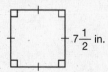

    $7\frac{1}{2}$ in.

Test 4–continued

11. (7) Look at the progression of the pattern below and formulate a conjecture regarding the number of squares there will be in the fifth step of this pattern.

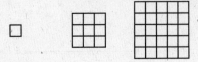

12. (10) Identify the hypothesis and conclusion of the conditional statement below.

   If $3x - 2 = 7$, then $x = 3$.

13. (2) Point Q lies on $\overline{PR}$ between P and R. $PQ = 7$ and $PR = 15$. Find QR.

14. (16) Write the equation of the line that has slope $\frac{1}{2}$ and passes through $(6, {}^-2)$.

15. (11) On the number line below, what is the midpoint of A and B?

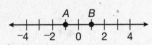

16. (20) Use a truth table to represent the statement, "If $x^2 \leq 49$, then $x \leq 7$." Interpret the table for this statement.

17. (13) In the diagram, which triangle is obtuse?

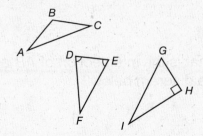

18. (5) In the figure below, $\overleftrightarrow{EF} \parallel \overleftrightarrow{GH}$, $\overleftrightarrow{AB} \perp \overleftrightarrow{GH}$, and $\overleftrightarrow{CD} \perp \overleftrightarrow{GH}$. What is the relationship between $\overleftrightarrow{AB}$ and $\overleftrightarrow{CD}$?

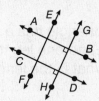

19. (8) Find the perimeter of a triangle with congruent side lengths all equal to 3.1 meters.

20. (4) Points X and Y lie on plane E. Does $\overleftrightarrow{XY}$ lie in plane E? Justify your answer using a postulate.

Homeschool Testing Book: Geometry SV 9781600329777

Test 5

1. *(21)* Use deductive reasoning to form a "Therefore" concluding statement from the given statements below.

   All members of the football team attended the awards banquet. Joe is a member of the football team.

2. *(23)* Name the circle. Identify a diameter, a radius, and the center of the circle.

   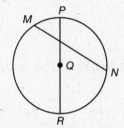

3. *(1)* Name three collinear points and three noncollinear points in the diagram below.

   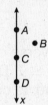

4. *(7)* Ben made the conjecture that the expression $2n + 1$ will always result in a prime number. Show that this conjecture is true for $n = 1, 2,$ and 3, but not for $n = 4$.

5. *(14)* Find a counterexample to the conjecture below.

   If a triangle is acute, then it is equiangular.

6. *(12)* Prove that lines *a* and *b* in this figure are parallel.

   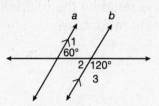

7. *(3)* m∠FEG = 7° and m∠GEH = 28°. Find m∠FEH. Classify ∠FEH.

8. *(22)* Find the area of the parallelogram below.

   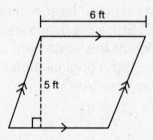

9. *(15)* For each numbered angle in the polygon, determine whether it is an interior angle or an exterior angle.

10. *(8)* Use the formula $F° = \frac{9}{5}(C°) + 32°$ to find the temperature in degrees Celsius when it is 86°F.

Test 5–continued

11. *(2)* Alice is biking up a mountain toward the summit. The distance from the base of the mountain to the summit is 2375 feet. How far will she have biked when she reaches the midpoint of her ride up the mountain?

12. *(25)* Identify the corresponding angles and sides for $\triangle LMN$ and $\triangle QRS$.

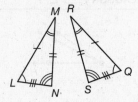

13. *(17)* Consider the conditional statement, "If Bill has a piano lesson, then it is a Monday." State the hypothesis and conclusion of this statement and write its converse. If the original statement is true, is the converse true?

14. *(18)* Find the measure of $\angle X$ in $\triangle XYZ$.

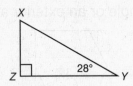

15. *(9)* Find the distance between the points on the number line.

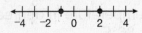

16. *(13)* A triangular horse corral has one side measuring 27.7 feet, a second side measuring 45.6 feet, and a third side measuring 39.5 feet. How much fencing is required to surround the corral?

17. *(24)* Solve the equation $3(x + 2) = x + 12$. Provide a justification for each step.

18. *(16)* Find the slope of the line below.

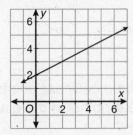

19. *(20)* State the converse of the statement *If $x^2 \le 49$, then $x \le 7$.* Determine whether the statement and its converse are true.

20. *(19)* Determine the perimeter and area of the rectangle below.

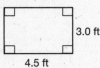

3.0 ft

4.5 ft

Homeschool Testing Book: Geometry SV 9781600329777

Name _____   Date _____

Test 6

1. *(21)* For the following statements, use the Law of Detachment to write a valid concluding statement.

   If an integer ends in 5, then it can be evenly divided by 5. The number 65 ends in 5.

2. *(22)* Find the area of the trapezoid below.

   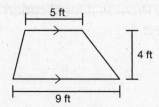

3. *(26)* Identify a central angle, minor arc, major arc, and semicircle in $\odot S$.

   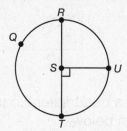

4. *(10)* Determine whether the statement below is true or false. If it is false, explain your reasoning.

   If an angle measures 115°, then it is obtuse.

5. *(14)* Find a counterexample to the conjecture below.

   If $x^2 = 25$, then $x = 5$.

6. *(Inv. 3)* Determine the measure of each exterior angle for a regular octagon.

7. *(25)* Write a congruence statement for the two triangles below.

   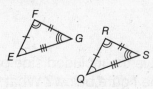

8. *(23)* Find the circumference of a circle with a radius of 2 feet. Use 3.14 for π and round to the nearest hundredth foot.

9. *(27)* Fill in the justifying statements to support the proof of Theorem 6-2: If two angles are supplementary to the same angle, then they are congruent.

   Given: ∠1 is supplementary to ∠2.
   ∠3 is supplementary to ∠2.

   Prove: ∠1 ≅ ∠3

Statements	Reasons
1. ∠1 is supplementary to ∠2. ∠3 is supplementary to ∠2.	1. Given
2. m∠1 + m∠2 = 180° m∠3 + m∠2 = 180°	2. _____
3. m∠1 + m∠2 = m∠3 + m∠2	3. _____
4. m∠1 + m∠2 − m∠2 = m∠3 + m∠2 − m∠2	4. _____
5. m∠1 = m∠3	5. _____
6. m∠1 ≅ m∠3	6. _____

10. *(2)* Identify the property that justifies the statement below.

    $\overline{CD} \cong \overline{EF}$ and $\overline{EF} \cong \overline{GH}$, so $\overline{CD} \cong \overline{GH}$.

Homeschool Testing Book: Geometry SV 9781600329777

Test 6–continued

11. *(7)* After years of eating peaches, Jacob made the observation that every peach he ate had a pit. He made this conjecture: "All peaches have pits." Is this a valid conjecture? How can it be tested? Can it be proven?

12. *(28)* What is the included side of ∠G and ∠H in the figure below? What is the included angle of $\overline{EF}$ and $\overline{FG}$?

13. *(17)* Identify the hypothesis and conclusion of the statement below. Then, write the negation of each.

If Liz goes to the mountains, then she goes skiing.

14. *(3)* Name three rays in the diagram below.

15. *(30)* Given that $\overline{AC} \cong \overline{ED}$, find the area of each triangle shown below.

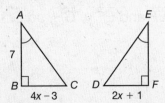

16. *(18)* In the right triangle CDE, m∠D = 34° and the right angle is at vertex E. Find the measure of ∠C.

17. *(24)* The area of a rectangular blanket is 20 square feet. The blanket's length is (2x + 1) feet and the blanket's width is 2x feet. Find the dimensions of the blanket. Provide a justification for each step.

18. *(29)* Find the value of x in the triangle below. Give your answer in simplified radical form.

19. *(19)* Sketch a quadrilateral based on the description below.

In quadrilateral ABCD, each side measures 7 centimeters. Also, all four angles are right angles.

20. *(8)* Find the base of a rectangle with an area of 48 square inches and a height of 6 inches.

Test 7

1. (34) A banner is shaped like a parallelogram with a diagonal of 4 feet, as shown. Calculate the values of *x* and *y* to the nearest hundredth.

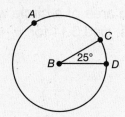

2. (26) What is m$\widehat{CD}$?

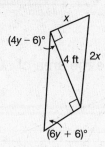

3. (30) Use ASA congruence to determine the measures of the sides of △*XYZ*.

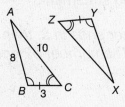

4. (22) Find the area of a parallelogram with a height of 6*x* and a base of 9*y*.

5. (11) Determine the midpoint *M* of the line segment $\overline{UV}$ with endpoints *U*(2, 7) and *V*(12, 8).

6. (27) Prove Theorem 6-3: If two angles form a linear pair, then they are supplementary.

   Given: ∠*ABD* and ∠*DBC* form a linear pair.

   Prove: ∠*ABD* and ∠*DBC* are supplementary.

7. (35) Find the arc length *L* of a circle with a radius of 16 feet and an arc measure of 45°. Give the answer in terms of π.

8. (18) For △*ABC*, determine the measure of ∠*ACD*.

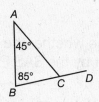

9. (17) Determine the contrapositive of the statement below.

   If Jason has a soccer game, then it is a Friday.

10. (31) Use the given flowchart to write a two-column proof.

   Given: ∠1 and ∠2 are supplementary.

   ∠2 and ∠3 are supplementary.

   Prove: ∠1 ≅ ∠3

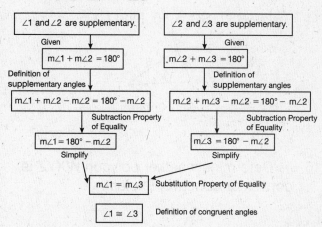

Test 7–continued

11. *(24)* The area of a rectangular tablecloth is 48 square feet. The tablecloth's length is $(6x - 10)$ feet, and the tablecloth's width is $2x$ feet. Find the dimensions of the tablecloth. Provide a justification for each step.

12. *(28)* Determine whether the pair of triangles is congruent by the SAS Postulate.

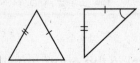

13. *(14)* Consider the following conjecture.

    If the product of two numbers is positive, then both numbers are positive.

    What is the hypothesis of the conjecture? What is its conclusion? Find a counterexample to the conjecture.

14. *(32)* In △RST, $SC = 15$. Find CX.

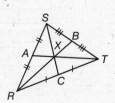

15. *(15)* Determine whether polygon *WXYZ* is convex or concave. Explain.

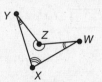

16. *(29)* Find the unknown length in the triangle below. Do the side lengths form a Pythagorean Triple?

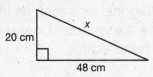

17. *(13)* Determine the area of △*CDE*.

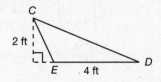

18. *(23)* Find the area of a circle with a radius of 7 inches. Use 3.14 for π.

19. *(21)* For the following statements, use the Law of Detachment to write a valid concluding statement.

    If an integer ends in 2, then it is an even number. The number 32 ends in 2.

20. *(33)* Find the value of x in the triangle below. Write your answer in simplified radical form.

Homeschool Testing Book: Geometry SV 9781600329777

Name _____   Date _____

Test 8

1. *(36)* Rosa must design a flag that will be exactly the same size as the triangle below. The flag will contain a right angle. Rosa knows that she only needs to pick two other dimensions to make sure that the flag is congruent to the triangle. List all the pairs of dimensions Rosa could use to ensure the flag is exactly the same size and shape as the triangle. For each pair of dimensions, write which triangle congruence theorem applies.

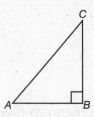

2. *(32)* Find the centroid of $\triangle EFG$ with vertices at $E(^-5, 5)$, $F(^-1, 3)$, and $G(^-3, 1)$.

3. *(23)* A circle has a diameter of 16 inches. What is the area of the circle to the nearest square inch? Use 3.14 for π.

4. *(37)* Are the lines $y = 3 + 5x$ and $y = 5x - 1$ parallel, perpendicular, or neither?

5. *(29)* Find the value of x in the triangle below. Give your answer in simplified radical form.

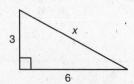

6. *(31)* Use the given paragraph proof to write a two-column proof.

Given: WXYZ is a quadrilateral.
∠W and ∠Z are right angles.

Prove: ∠X and ∠Y are supplementary angles.

WXYZ is a quadrilateral, and ∠W and ∠Z are right angles. So, m∠W = 90° and m∠Z = 90° by the definition of a right angle. By the Formula for the Sum of the Interior Angles of a Polygon, m∠W + m∠X + m∠Y + m∠Z = 360°. By the Subtraction Property of Equality, m∠W + m∠X + m∠Y + m∠Z − (m∠W + m∠Z) = 360° − (m∠W + m∠Z).

So, m∠X + m∠Y = 180°. Therefore, ∠X and ∠Y are supplementary angles by the definition of supplementary angles.

7. *(28)* What is the included angle of $\overrightarrow{EF}$ and $\overrightarrow{EG}$?

8. *(33)* Determine whether the triangle below is a right triangle.

9. *(39)* Decide whether each set of side lengths could form a valid triangle: (6, 8, 9), (3, 8, 5), and (4, 9, 14).

10. *(21)* Use the Law of Syllogism to write a valid set of conditional statements for the following three statements in the form "If p, then q. If q, then r. If p, then r."

p: The zoo is open.
q: Leo can go to the zoo.
r: Leo can see a zebra.

Test 8–continued

11. *(40)* The diagram shows the floor of a kitchen. What area of linoleum will be needed to cover the floor?

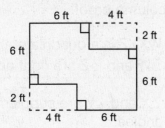

12. *(22)* A rectangular mirror has a length of 9.5 inches and a width of 7.5 inches. What is the area of the mirror?

13. *(20)* Write the biconditional of the statement and its converse.

If $x^2 \leq 169$, then $x \leq 13$.

Is it true? Explain why or why not.

14. *(25)* For $\triangle LMN$, $LM = 20$, $MN = 15$, and $LN = 25$. For $\triangle EFG$, $EF = 20$, $EG = 15$, and $FG = 25$. Write the congruency statement for the triangles.

15. *(18)* In the right triangle JKL, $\angle J$ measures $22°$ and the right angle is at vertex K. Find m$\angle L$.

16. *(17)* Write the inverse of the statement below. Is the statement true? Is the inverse of the statement true?

If the measure of an angle is 90°, then the angle is a right angle.

17. *(34)* WXYZ is a parallelogram. Find the value of x.

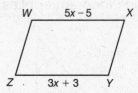

18. *(38)* Using the diagram below, find FG if $EH = 16$, $GH = 8$, and $EF = 15$.

19. *(24)* Solve the equation below. Provide a justification for each step.

$3(x - 4) = x + 2$

20. *(Inv. 4)* Compare the measures of $\overline{UW}$ and $\overline{XZ}$.

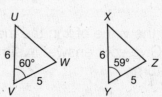

Homeschool Testing Book: Geometry SV 9781600329777

Test 9

1. *(23)* A ribbon surrounds the edge of a circular hat that has a radius of 8 inches. Find the length of the ribbon to the nearest tenth inch. Use 3.14 for π.

2. *(37)* Find a line that is parallel to $y = x + 7$ and passes through the point (2, 4).

3. *(20)* State the converse of this statement: *If a quadrilateral is a square, then it is a rhombus.* Determine whether the original statement and its converse are true.

4. *(40)* Find the perimeter of the composite figure below.

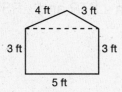

5. *(30)* Write a two-column proof to prove that $\triangle EDF \cong \triangle GHF$ given that F is a midpoint of $\overline{DH}$ and $\overleftrightarrow{DE} \parallel \overleftrightarrow{GH}$.

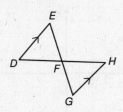

6. *(42)* Find the distance from the point P (5, 3) to the line $x = 7$.

7. *(44)* The pentagons in the diagram are similar. Find the values of x and y.

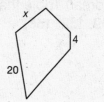

8. *(41)* Consider $\triangle ABC$ and $\triangle DEF$ shown below. Write a proportion to show that $AB : DE = BC : EF$.

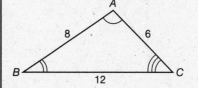 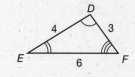

9. *(32)* In triangle XYZ, $\overline{XA}$ is a median, and M is the centroid of the triangle. What is the length of $\overline{XM}$ if $\overline{XA}$ measures 163.2 centimeters?

10. *(33)* A triangle has side lengths that measure 15, 8, and 12 units. Classify the triangle by side lengths and angles.

 Homeschool Testing Book: Geometry SV 9781600329777

Test 9—continued

11. (24) A triangular scarf has an area of 36 square inches. The base of the scarf measures $3x$ inches and the height measures $2x + 2$ inches. Find the base and height measurements of the scarf. Provide a justification for each step.

12. (29) Give a Pythagorean Triple that is proportional to (99, 132, 165).

13. (36) Use the LA Congruence Theorem to prove that $\triangle ABC$ and $\triangle DEF$ are congruent.

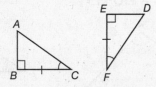

14. (38) A library has three branches located throughout a city at points $D(1, 3)$, $E(1, 1)$, and $F(5, 1)$. The main library is equidistant from the three branches. Find the location of the main library.

15. (43) Name a tangent line to the circle shown below and identify the point of tangency.

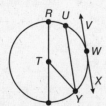

16. (Inv. 3) What is the sum of the interior angle measures of a convex, irregular pentagon?

17. (34) In the parallelogram shown, what are the measures of $\angle TQR$, $\angle QRS$, and $\angle SRU$?

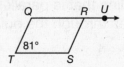

18. (39) Order the lengths of $\triangle XYZ$ from least to greatest.

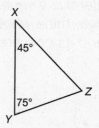

19. (28) What is the included side of $\triangle RST$ that is between $\angle STR$ and $\angle RST$?

20. (45) Triangle DEF has a base of 2 units and a height of 2 units. Angle D is a right angle. Position $\triangle DEF$ on the coordinate plane.

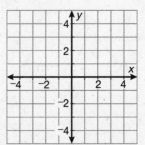

Name _____ Date _____

Test 10

1. (42) A school only provides bus service to students who live a distance greater than 2 miles away from the school. On a coordinate plane, the school is located at the origin, and Michael lives at the closest point to the school on Maple Street, which can be represented by the line $y = 2x - 4$. If each unit on the coordinate plane represents 1 mile, does Michael live far enough from the school for bus service?

2. (33) Find the value of x in the diagram below. Write your answer in simplified radical form.

3. (26) The measure of $\overarc{AB}$ is given by the expression $4x + 10$ and the measure of $\overarc{XY}$ is given by the expression $6x - 20$. It is given that $\overarc{AB} \cong \overarc{XY}$. Determine the value of x and the measure of each arc.

4. (41) Solve the proportion $\frac{20}{25} = \frac{x}{45}$ to find the value of x.

5. (37) Are the lines $y = 5x - 1$ and $y = 2 + 5x$ parallel, perpendicular, or neither?

6. (48) Write an indirect proof to prove Theorem 4-2: If there is a line and a point not on the line, then exactly one plane contains them.

7. (35) Find the area of sector AOB with radius 24 feet and m$\overarc{AOB}$ = 75°. Give your answer in terms of π.

8. (28) What is the included side of $\angle S$ and $\angle U$ in the triangle below? What is the included angle of $\overline{SU}$ and $\overline{ST}$?

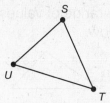

9. (29) Find the unknown length x in the triangle below. Do the side lengths form a Pythagorean Triple?

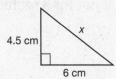

10. (46) Show that the two triangles below are similar if $\overline{VW} \parallel \overline{YZ}$. Then find YZ.

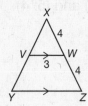

Test 10—continued

11. *(49)* Classify the three-dimensional solid shown below.

12. *(43)* Find the length *x* in the diagram below.

13. *(39)* Find the range of values for *x* in the triangle below.

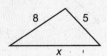

14. *(Inv. 5)* Draw a net for a rectangular prism.

15. *(16)* Determine the slope of the line passing through (2, 7) and (5, 4).

16. *(44)* Given that △*DEF* ~ △*JKL,* prove algebraically that the ratio of their perimeters is 1 : 3 if the ratio of their corresponding sides is 1 : 3.

17. *(47)* Name the inscribed angle shown in the circle below.

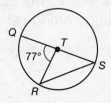

18. *(45)* Assign coordinates to the vertices of isosceles triangle *DEF* with a height of 6 from the base to the vertex.

19. *(50)* Find the geometric mean of 2 and 8.

20. *(40)* Find the perimeter of the composite figure below.

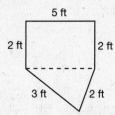

Homeschool Testing Book: Geometry SV 9781600329777

Test 11

1. (44) An interior decorator is buying fringe for the edge of a rug in the shape of a regular octagon. The side length of the rug measures $\frac{1}{2}$ inch on a diagram with the scale 1 inch : 4 feet. How many feet of fringe will be needed for the entire edge of the rug?

2. (43) Find m∠OCA in the diagram below.

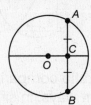

3. (51) A triangle is equiangular and has a perimeter of 16.5 inches. Determine the length of each side.

4. (39) Order the measures of the angles in triangle ABC from least to greatest.

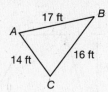

5. (54) Draw a pentagonal prism in one-point perspective. Use a pencil with an eraser.

6. (46) Given the two triangles with values as shown below, show that they are similar triangles.

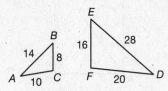

7. (35) Find the arc length of $\overset{\frown}{XY}$ in the circle with radius 8 centimeters and m$\overset{\frown}{XY}$ = 90°. Give your answer in terms of π.

8. (49) How many faces does a polyhedron with 4 vertices and 6 edges have?

9. (50) Find WZ and WX in the diagram below.

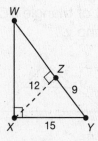

10. (48) Write an indirect proof to prove Theorem 39-2: If one angle of a triangle is larger than another angle, then the side opposite the first angle is longer than the side opposite the second angle.

    Given: For △WXY, m∠X > m∠Y
    Prove: WY > WX

Test 11—continued

11. *(52)* A rectangular frame is divided by diagonal edges as shown below. If PI is 5 in. long, what is the length of $\overline{QR}$?

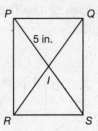

12. *(42)* Find the distance from point $P(8, 9)$ to the line $x = 5$.

13. *(38)* Using the diagram below, find XY if $WZ = 24$, $YZ = 8$, and $WX = 20$.

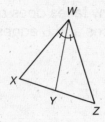

14. *(55)* In the diagram below, $\overline{MN}$ is a midsegment of triangle PQR. Find the values of x and y.

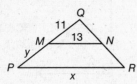

15. *(45)* Triangle PQR has vertices $P(0, 0)$, $Q(2, 0)$, and $R(1, 3)$. Use a coordinate proof to show that triangle PQR is an isosceles triangle.

16. *(20)* A museum has members and non-members. The museum store gives discounts on all purchases to museum members. Consider the statements "a customer is a museum member," and "a customer gets a discount." What is the conjunction of these statements? Use a truth table to assess its truth.

17. *(47)* Find the measure of $\angle 1$, $\angle 2$, and $\angle 3$ in the diagram below.

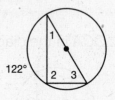

18. *(41)* Write the ratio comparing TU to XY in three different ways, in simplest form.

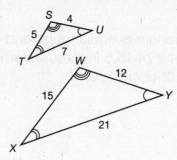

19. *(22)* Find the area of the trapezoid below.

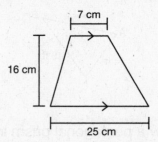

20. *(53)* Find the exact length of the hypotenuse of a 45°-45°-90° right triangle if one leg measures 13 centimeters.

Test 12

Name _____   **Date** _____

1. *(42)* Find the distance from point $P(3, -1)$ to the line $y = 5$.

2. *(56)* Find the values of x and y in the diagram below. Give your answer in simplified radical form.

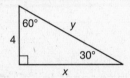

3. *(55)* Triangle *EFG* has vertices $E(-1, 3)$, $F(3, 4)$, and $G(2, 1)$ as shown below. $\overline{CD}$ is a midsegment of $\triangle EFG$. Find the coordinates of *C* and *D*.

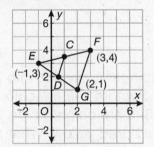

4. *(51)* Triangle *ABC* is isosceles, and its vertex angle is at *B*. If $m\angle A = 25°$, determine $m\angle B$ and $m\angle C$.

5. *(40)* Find the area of the shaded region in the figure below.

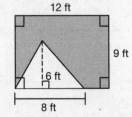

6. *(45)* Cassie is building a patio next to her rectangular garden. She draws a diagram of what she plans to build and overlays a coordinate grid on it as shown below. Prove that the patio has an area that is one-fourth the size of the garden's area.

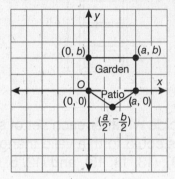

7. *(60)* Find *WV*.

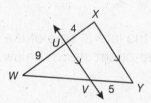

8. *(54)* Draw a triangular prism in two-point perspective in which the vanishing points are above the prism.

9. *(57)* Find the perimeter of rectangle *WXYZ* with coordinates $W(3, 7)$, $X(3, -1)$, $Y(6, -1)$, and $Z(6, 7)$.

10. *(43)* The circle shown has a diameter of 22 inches. Chord $\overline{BD}$ is 8 inches long. How far is $\overline{BD}$ from the center of the circle?

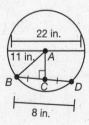

Homeschool Testing Book: Geometry SV 9781600329777

Test 12—continued

11. *(52)* The rectangular bookcase shown below has braces placed diagonally across the back. Determine the length of the brace that will be used for diagonal $\overline{WY}$.

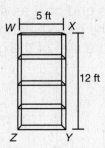

12. *(39)* Decide whether each set of side lengths could form a valid triangle: (5, 4, 9), (13, 14, 15), and (12, 5, 6).

13. *(59)* Find the lateral area of the regular triangular prism shown below.

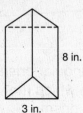

14. *(50)* Find the geometric mean of 3 and 24 to the nearest tenth.

15. *(44)* The pentagons in the diagram below are similar. Find x and y.

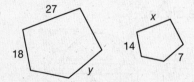

16. *(46)* Prove that $\triangle DEF \sim \triangle GHF$ as shown in the diagram below.

17. *(41)* Solve the proportion $\dfrac{9}{54} = \dfrac{x}{72}$.

18. *(58)* Line p is tangent to $\odot C$ at A, and line q passes through C. Lines p and q intersect at B. If $m\angle CBA = 25°$, determine $m\angle ACB$.

19. *(Inv. 6)* A spinner is divided into 8 equal sectors. Sectors 1–2 are colored red, sectors 3–5 are colored blue, and sectors 6–8 are colored yellow. What are the measures of the red, blue, and yellow central angles?

20. *(53)* Find the perimeter of the triangle to the nearest hundredth foot.

Test 13

1. (35) A water sprinkler rotates 210° through a circle that has a radius of 24 feet. What is the area that the sprinkler covers? Round to the nearest square foot.

2. (51) A triangle is equiangular and has a perimeter of 38.4 centimeters. Determine the length of each side.

3. (44) Figures *ABCD* and *WXYZ* are similar polygons. Their corresponding sides have a ratio of 4 : 5. If the perimeter of figure *ABCD* is 38 inches, what is the perimeter of figure *WXYZ*?

4. (55) In the diagram below, $\overline{ST}$ is a midsegment of △*WXY*. Find the values of *a* and *b*.

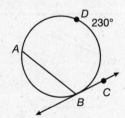

5. (64) Find m∠*ABC* in the figure below, given that $\overline{BC}$ is a tangent.

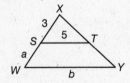

6. (58) If m∠*DHE* = 45° in the diagram below, prove that $\overleftrightarrow{DG}$ is tangent to ⊙*F*.

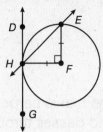

7. (61) In quadrilateral *QRST* shown below, $\overline{QR} \parallel \overline{TS}$ and ∠*T* ≅ ∠*R*. Is *QRST* a parallelogram?

8. (59) Find the volume of a right prism if the base is a 3-foot-by-7-foot rectangle and the height is 4 feet.

9. (22) Find the area of the parallelogram if the height is 6 feet and the base is 9 feet.

10. (65) Is the parallelogram below a rhombus if *x* = 5? Explain.

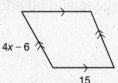

Homeschool Testing Book: Geometry SV 9781600329777

Test 13—continued

11. *(56)* A silk scarf is in the shape of an equilateral triangle and each side measures 20 inches. What is the area of the scarf? Give your answer in simplified radical form.

12. *(37)* Find a line that is perpendicular to $y = -\frac{1}{2}x$ and passes through point (4, 6).

13. *(62)* Find the lateral area of the cylinder shown below in terms of π.

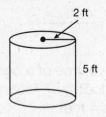

14. *(41)* Find the unknown side lengths in the two similar triangles below.

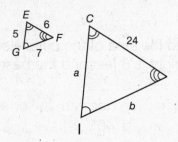

15. *(49)* How many faces does a polyhedron with 20 vertices and 30 edges have?

16. *(60)* Is $\overline{JK}$ parallel to $\overline{FG}$ in the diagram below?

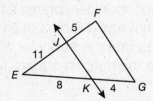

17. *(57)* Find the perimeter of rectangle ABCD with coordinates A(1, 3), B(2, 1), C(−2, −1), and D(−3, 1). Give your answer in simplified radical form.

18. *(33)* Determine whether a triangle with sides 5, 8, and 9 is a right triangle.

19. *(21)* For the statement set below, draw a valid conclusion. Identify which law is used to reach the conclusion.

If Carlos is hungry, he goes to the supermarket. If Carlos goes to the supermarket, he buys food.

20. *(63)* Name each vector shown in the diagram below. Identify the terminal points of each vector, if applicable.

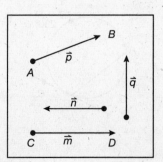

Name _____ Date _____

Test 14

1. *(66)* Find the perimeter of a regular pentagon if one side is 7 feet long.

2. *(64)* Find b in the diagram below.

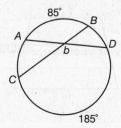

3. *(37)* Write the equation of a line that is parallel to $y = x + 1$ and passes through point (4, 8).

4. *(68)* Give the sine, cosine, and tangent of $\angle E$ in the triangle below.

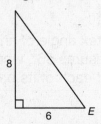

5. *(60)* In the diagram below, $\overrightarrow{AB}$, $\overrightarrow{CD}$, and $\overrightarrow{EF}$ are parallel. Find the length of $\overline{AC}$.

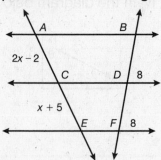

6. *(65)* Is parallelogram *ABCD* shown below a rectangle?

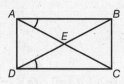

7. *(62)* Find the total surface area of a right cylinder in terms of π if the height is 11 centimeters and the radius is 12 centimeters.

8. *(61)* A road surrounds the perimeter of the park shown below. The park has two bike paths that bisect each other to form an "X." What is the length of the road?

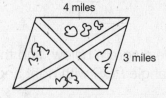

9. *(Inv. 7)* In $\triangle DEF$, $\angle D$ is a right angle, $m\angle E = 60°$, and $DF = 6$. How are *DE* and *EF* related? Determine *DE* and *EF*. Then, give exact values for $\sin 60°$, $\cos 60°$, and $\tan 60°$.

10. *(59)* Find the volume of the oblique prism shown below.

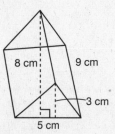

Test 14—continued

11. (53) A square rug has a diagonal length of 12 feet. What is the square footage of the rug?

12. (70) What is the lateral area of a regular hexagonal pyramid with a side length of 6 meters and a slant length of 8 meters?

13. (67) Identify the type of transformation illustrated below.

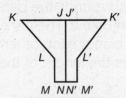

14. (57) In the diagram below, find the area of right triangle PQR with right angle ∠PRQ.

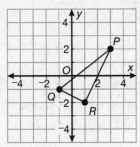

15. (50) Find the geometric mean of 5 and 22 to the nearest tenth.

16. (42) Find the distance from point A(9, 5) to the line y = 2.

17. (69) The midsegment of trapezoid DEFG shown below is $\overline{XY}$. Find the length of $\overline{XY}$.

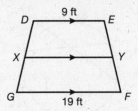

18. (58) In the figure below, $\overline{AB}$ and $\overline{AD}$ are tangent to ⊙C. Determine the perimeter of quadrilateral ABCD. What type of quadrilateral is ABCD?

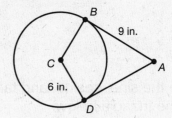

19. (51) If the vertex angle of an isosceles triangle measures 56°, what are the measures of each of its base angles?

20. (63) Find |$\vec{v}$| in the diagram below.

Homeschool Testing Book: Geometry SV 9781600329777

Test 15

1. (62) A flour canister is in the shape of a cylinder with a height of 14 inches and a radius of 5 inches. How many cubic inches of flour can the canister hold? Use 3.14 for π.

2. (69) Find the measures of $\angle B$, $\angle C$, and $\angle D$ in trapezoid $ABCD$.

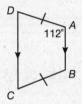

3. (71) A square has vertices $E(4, 4)$, $F(7, 4)$, $G(7, 7)$, and $H(4, 7)$. It is translated 5 units to the right. What are the coordinates of E', F', G', and H'?

4. (63) Add vectors $\vec{p}$ and $\vec{q}$ in the diagram below.

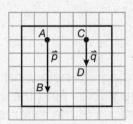

5. (67) Reflect the figure shown below across $\overleftrightarrow{DE}$.

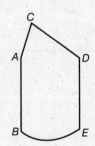

6. (56) Find the perimeter of the triangle shown below. Give your answer in simplified radical form.

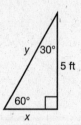

7. (66) Use the apothem and perimeter to find the area of a regular hexagon with side length 12 feet.

8. (52) A rectangular painting has diagonal braces as shown below. If EA is 7 feet long, what is the length of $\overline{FH}$?

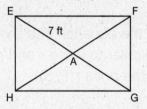

9. (68) Use a calculator to evaluate the expression cos27°. Round the answer to the nearest hundredth.

10. (72) In the diagram below, $\overleftrightarrow{JM}$ and $\overleftrightarrow{KL}$ are internal common tangents to $\odot M$ and $\odot N$. Find the lengths of $\overline{JP}$ and $\overline{KP}$.

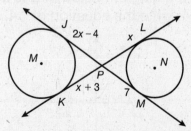

11. *(73)* In the diagram below, use the angle of elevation between the radio antenna and the person to find the horizontal distance between the antenna and the person, and the height of the antenna.

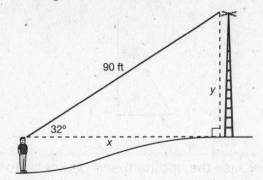

12. *(70)* Calculate the surface area of a regular hexagonal pyramid with a slant height of 9 meters and a base side length of 4 meters.

13. *(37)* Write the equation of a line that is perpendicular to $y = \frac{5}{6}x$ and passes through the point (15, 3).

14. *(59)* Find the volume of a right prism where the base is a 2-foot-by-3-foot rectangle and the height is 7 feet.

15. *(75)* In the diagram below, if *B* is a point on $\odot A$, write the equation of $\odot A$.

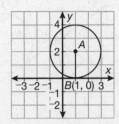

16. *(57)* Find the perimeter of rectangle *EFGH* with coordinates $E(^-1, 4)$, $F(6, 4)$, $G(6, ^-1)$, and $H(^-1, ^-1)$.

17. *(53)* Find the perimeter of the triangle shown below.

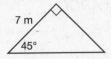

18. *(39)* Order the sides of △*XYZ* from least to greatest.

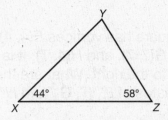

19. *(51)* The perimeter of △*JKL* is 32 inches, and $\angle J \cong \angle K$. If $\overline{JK} = 12$ inches, determine the length of segment *JL*.

20. *(74)* In the diagram below, reflect △*DEF* across the *y*-axis. Find the coordinates of the vertices of the reflected image and write the transformation in mapping notation.

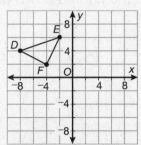

Test 16

1. (73) A person on top of a 50-meter water tower sees a car below. If the angle of depression from the top of the water tower to the car below is 30°, how far is the person from the car?

2. (72) In the diagram, ⊙J is tangent to ⊙L, and $\overline{KM}$ is tangent to ⊙J. The radius of ⊙J is 8 meters and the radius of ⊙L is 6 meters. Find the area of △JMK to the nearest square meter.

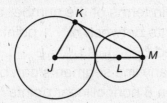

3. (78) If △ABC has vertices A(3, 4), B(1, 3), and C(4, 1), graph the triangle and its rotation 180° counterclockwise about the origin.

4. (65) Is the parallelogram shown below a rectangle?

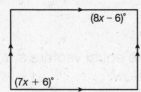

5. (76) Identify whether the figure below has a line of symmetry. If it does, draw the line of symmetry.

6. (67) Identify the type of transformation illustrated below.

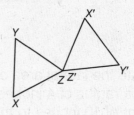

7. (75) The equation of ⊙A is $x^2 + y^2 = 49$. Graph ⊙A.

8. (79) Find m∠R in the diagram below.

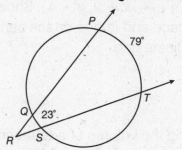

9. (68) Use a calculator to evaluate the expression sin 72°. Round to the nearest hundredth.

10. (64) In the diagram below, find m∠WXY given that $\overleftrightarrow{XY}$ is a tangent.

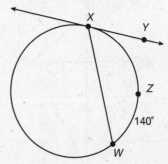

Test 16–continued

11. *(66)* Mary is painting the floor of a gazebo that is in the shape of a regular hexagon with 12-foot side lengths. What is the total area that must be painted?

12. *(77)* Calculate the lateral area of a right cone with a radius of 4 inches and a slant height of 10 inches to the nearest hundredth square inch.

13. *(71)* The vertices of a triangle are $A(-1, 0)$, $B(-3, -3)$, and $C(2, -2)$. Find the image of $\triangle EFG$ after the translation $T:(x, y) \rightarrow (x + 2, y + 4)$. Show the preimage and image on the same coordinate grid.

14. *(70)* Find the volume of a tetrahedron, a regular triangular pyramid where all faces are congruent, with a base area of 6.6 square centimeters and a height of 3.25 centimeters.

15. *(69)* Find the lengths of the sides of kite $ABCD$ shown below. Round to the nearest tenth.

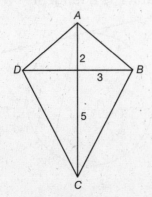

16. *(80)* Find the surface area of a sphere with a 3-foot radius in terms of π.

17. *(62)* Find the lateral area of a cylinder with a radius of 10 inches and a height of 15 inches in terms of π.

18. *(Inv. 8)* The rule for the number of line segments, L, between n noncollinear points, in terms of the number of line segments between $n - 1$ points (denoted L_{n-1}), is $L_n = L_{n-1} + (n - 1)$. How many line segments can be drawn between 8 noncollinear points?

19. *(74)* Rectangle $ABCD$ has vertices at $A(-4, 6)$, $B(2, 6)$, $C(2, 4)$, and $D(-4, 4)$. Reflect $ABCD$ across the line $y = 3$. Identify the coordinates of the vertices of the reflected image.

20. *(63)* Add the equal vectors $\vec{s}$, $\vec{t}$, and $\vec{u}$ shown below.

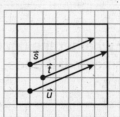

Homeschool Testing Book: Geometry SV 9781600329777

Name _____ Date _____

Test 17

1. (73) A helicopter is hovering in the air 200 feet off the ground. Louis sees the helicopter at an angle of elevation of 55°. Theresa sees the helicopter at an angle of elevation of 40°. Who is farther away from the helicopter? Explain.

2. (82) In the diagram below, find θ to the nearest degree.

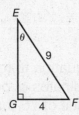

3. (77) Calculate the surface area of a cone with a slant height of 7 inches and a base radius of 5 inches, in terms of π.

4. (76) Tell whether the figure below has rotational symmetry. If so, give the angle of rotational symmetry and the order.

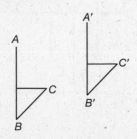

5. (67) Identify the type of transformation illustrated below.

6. (74) Rectangle ABCD has vertices at $A(^-4, 3)$, $B(^-6, 3)$, $C(^-6, 6)$, and $D(^-4, 6)$. Reflect ABCD across the line $y = x$. Identify the coordinates of the vertices of the reflection image.

7. (81) Solve the system of equations below algebraically.

$$y = -\frac{1}{4}x + 3 \qquad y = \frac{3}{2}x - 4$$

8. (68) Use a calculator to evaluate the expression tan 25°. Round the answer to the nearest hundredth.

9. (83) Use the parallelogram method to add the two vectors below.

$$\vec{a} = \langle 1, 3 \rangle \text{ and } \vec{b} = \langle 3, ^-1 \rangle$$

10. (72) A machine has a system of two pulleys and a belt as shown below. Find the length of the belt between A and C, B and D, and D and E.

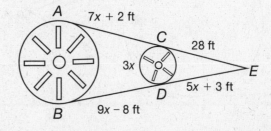

Homeschool Testing Book: Geometry SV 9781600329777

Test 17—continued

11. (71) A car in an animated cartoon will move from the point (6, −2) through the translations $a = \langle 9, 4 \rangle$ and $b = \langle -2, -5 \rangle$. What are the positions of the car after each translation?

12. (84) In the diagram below, apply a dilation to $\overline{BC}$ using a scale factor of 2 and center A.

13. (80) Find the volume of a sphere with a radius of 12 feet.

14. (66) Find the area of an equilateral triangle with a side length of 30 meters.

15. (79) Find m∠D in the diagram below.

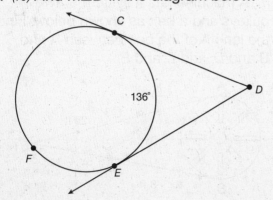

16. (69) In isosceles trapezoid PQRS shown below, find the length of $\overline{PT}$ if QS = 22.3 feet and ST = 16.9 feet.

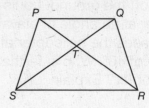

17. (78) Rotate the point (−3, 2) 90° counterclockwise around the center of rotation (−3, 4).

18. (75) Write an equation to relate all the x- and y-coordinates of points that lie on ⊙C with a radius of $\sqrt{5}$ that is centered at the origin.

19. (70) What is the lateral area of a regular hexagonal pyramid with a side length of 12 feet and a slant length of 17 feet?

20. (85) In the diagram below, if the plane is perpendicular to the prism's altitude, what figure is the cross section?

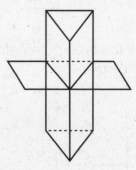

Homeschool Testing Book: Geometry SV 9781600329777

Test 18

1. *(83)* A hot air balloon has traveled a horizontal distance that can be represented by the vector $\langle 3000, 0 \rangle$, and a vertical distance that can be represented by the vector $\langle 0, 500 \rangle$, where the magnitude of both vectors is measured in feet. What is the magnitude of the distance the balloon has traveled?

2. *(86)* In the circle below, chords $\overline{EF}$ and $\overline{GH}$ intersect at X. Determine FX.

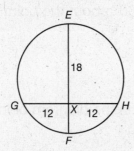

3. *(81)* Solve the linear system below by graphing.

$$y = \frac{1}{2}x - 4 \qquad y = -\frac{3}{2}x + 4$$

4. *(76)* Does the flower below have any lines of symmetry? If so, how many?

5. *(82)* In the diagram below, find θ to the nearest degree.

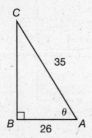

6. *(68)* In the diagram below, use the tangent function to find b to the nearest hundredth.

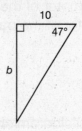

7. *(77)* An ice cream cone has a radius of 1.2 inches and a height of 6.5 inches. What is the volume of the ice cream cone?

8. *(75)* Write an equation to relate all the x- and y-coordinates of points that lie on a radius of 6, which is centered at the origin.

9. *(Inv. 9)* In a tessellation of regular hexagons, how many hexagons meet at each vertex of the tessellation? What is the measure of each vertex of the hexagon? What is the total angle measure of all the angles that meet at a vertex?

10. *(87)* In the similar figures below, the perimeter of the smaller rectangle is 24 feet. Determine the perimeter of the larger shape.

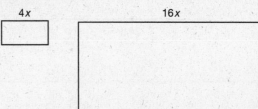

Test 18-continued

11. (84) An artist is making a sketch for a painting. The sketch measures 8 inches by 12 inches. If the painting will be 175% the size of the sketch, what will be the lengths of the sides of the painting? How does the perimeter of the sketch compare to the perimeter of the painting?

12. (65) Is the parallelogram shown below a rhombus if $x = 7$?

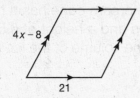

13. (88) Solve the strict linear inequality $5x + 3y > 4$ for y.

14. (66) Find the perimeter of a regular pentagon with a side length of 8.9 meters.

15. (69) The midsegment of trapezoid QRST shown below is $\overline{UV}$. Find the length of $\overline{UV}$.

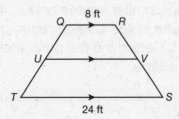

16. (90) Reflect △DEF across the line m and then translate it along $\vec{v}$.

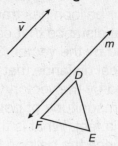

17. (78) Triangle ABC has vertices at A(2, 1), B(4, 2), and C(1, 4). What would be the coordinates of the image if △ABC were rotated 180° about the point D(1, 1)?

18. (64) Find x in the diagram below.

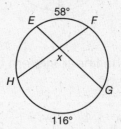

19. (89) Decompose the vector ⟨3, 5⟩.

20. (85) If the plane shown below is perpendicular to the altitude of the cylinder, what is the perimeter of the cross section?

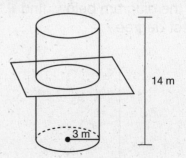

Homeschool Testing Book: Geometry SV 9781600329777

Test 19

1. (73) From the ground 30 feet away from a tree, the angle of elevation to the top of the tree is 38°. Find the height of the tree to the nearest foot.

2. (80) Find the surface area and volume of a hemisphere with an 18-inch diameter.

3. (91) Find sin θ if cos θ = 0.67.

4. (83) Add the vectors $\vec{e} = \langle 6, 4 \rangle$, $\vec{f} = \langle -2, 2 \rangle$, and $\vec{g} = \langle -1, -1 \rangle$.

5. (93) Draw the front, top, and side views of the solid below.

6. (92) The vertices of quadrilateral QRST are Q(9, 3), R(4, 1), S(1, 3), and T(6, 5). Is QRST a parallelogram?

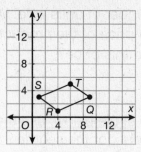

7. (88) Graph the inequality $y < \frac{1}{2}x - 2$.

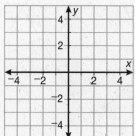

8. (66) A tile is in the shape of an equilateral triangle with 6-inch sides. What is the area of the tile?

9. (71) A horse in a computer animation will move from the point (−3, −4) through the translations $\vec{p} = \langle 6, 8 \rangle$ and $\vec{q} = \langle -1, 5 \rangle$. What are the positions of the horse after each translation?

10. (94) Find the length of $\overline{AC}$.

Test 19–continued

11. (81) The supply curve for a product is represented by the function $y = \frac{1}{2}x + 35$ and the demand curve is represented by the function $y = -\frac{1}{5}x + 56$, where y is the price of the product in dollars and x is the number of units sold. What is the optimum price of the product? How many will sell at this price?

12. (86) In the circle below, use the expressions for the segment lengths to write and solve an equation for x.

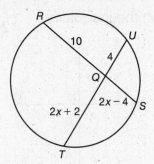

13. (95) The equation of a circle is $(x - 4)^2 + (y - 3)^2 = 9$. What is the equation of the circle if it is translated 7 units to the left and 3 units down?

14. (75) The equation of $\odot C$ is $(x + 2)^2 + (y - 1)^2 = 16$. If $\odot D$ is concentric with $\odot C$ and has a radius of 3, what is the equation of $\odot D$?

15. (84) Apply a dilation to $\triangle EFG$ using a scale factor of $\frac{1}{2}$ and center H.

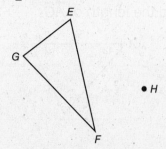

16. (82) In the diagram below, find θ to the nearest tenth of a degree.

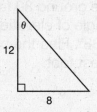

17. (57) Find the perimeter of rectangle $EFGH$ with coordinates $E(^-3, ^-2)$, $F(^-8, ^-2)$, $G(^-8, 9)$, and $H(^-3, 9)$.

18. (87) The two triangles shown below have a similarity ratio of 3 : 5. Determine the ratio of their areas and the area of the smaller triangle.

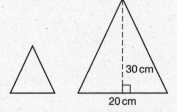

19. (89) $\vec{V}$ makes a 22° angle with the horizontal and has a magnitude of 6. Decompose the vector. Round to the nearest hundredth.

20. (85) Describe the cross section of the solid below.

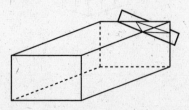

Homeschool Testing Book: Geometry SV 9781600329777

Test 20

1. *(84)* A 2-inch-by-4-inch photograph negative is enlarged 250% to make a photographic print. What will be the lengths of the sides of the print? How does the perimeter of the original photograph negative compare to the perimeter of the print?

2. *(97)* Determine whether the two circles in the diagram below are concentric. Explain your reasoning.

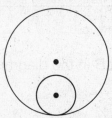

3. *(86)* In ⊙M, chords $\overline{QR}$ and $\overline{ST}$ intersect at U. Determine TU if QU = 5, RU = 9, and SU = 10.

4. *(100)* Add the two matrices below.

$$\begin{bmatrix} 2 & 0 \\ 5 & -4 \end{bmatrix} + \begin{bmatrix} -1 & 4 \\ 0 & 2 \end{bmatrix}$$

5. *(87)* On a floor plan, a porch in the shape of a trapezoid has an area of 1.25 square feet. If the floor plan has a scale of 1 : 12, what will be the actual area of the porch when it is built?

6. *(94)* Find the measure of ∠A in the triangle below. Round your answer to the nearest degree.

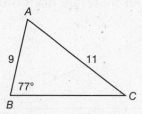

7. *(82)* In the diagram below, find θ to the nearest degree.

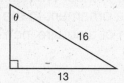

8. *(96)* A rectangle is one-half as tall as it is long. If its height is reduced to one-fourth its current height, what is the ratio of the new rectangle's perimeter to the original rectangle's perimeter?

9. *(83)* Add the vectors $\vec{a} = \langle 0, 5 \rangle$ and $\vec{b} = \langle 8, 0 \rangle$, and find the magnitude and angle from the horizontal of the resultant vector.

10. *(98)* Find c in the diagram below. Round your answer to the nearest tenth.

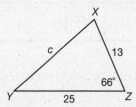

11. (91) Rico and Jane are standing on a bike path looking at a tree as shown in the diagram below. Jane is four times as far from the tree as Rico is. What is the approximate ratio of Jane's distance from Rico to her distance from the tree?

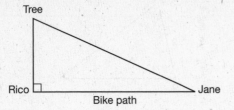

12. (80) A spherical lawn ornament has a radius of 8 inches. What is the surface area of the ornament to the nearest hundredth of a square inch?

13. (99) The two similar rectangular pyramids shown below have a scale factor of 5 : 4. Determine the perimeter of the smaller pyramid's base.

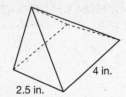
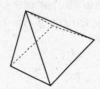

14. (95) The equation of a circle is $x^2 + y^2 = 4$. Apply a dilation centered at the origin with a scale factor of 2. What is the new equation of the circle?

15. (Inv. 10) The diagram below shows the first two iterations of a fractal pattern. Draw the third iteration.

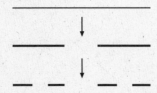

16. (81) Determine whether there is a solution for the system of linear equations below. If not, explain why not.

$$y = 2x + 5$$
$$2y + 2 = 4x - 4$$
$$y = \frac{4}{2}x + 1$$

17. (92) Is quadrilateral EFGH a trapezoid?

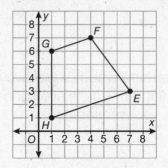

18. (79) Find m∠B in the diagram below.

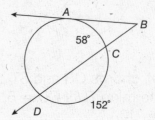

19. (88) Solve the strict inequality $3x - 2y < 7$ for y.

20. (93) A building in the shape of a rectangular prism is 60 feet along the front, 30 feet along the side, and 120 feet high. A penthouse in the shape of a rectangular prism is 20 feet along the front, 30 feet along the side, and 20 feet high. Make orthographic drawings of the front, side, and top of the building.

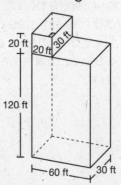

Name _____   Date _____

Test 21

1. *(94)* Two football players are 35 feet apart as shown in the diagram below. How far is each player from the football? Find the distance to the nearest foot.

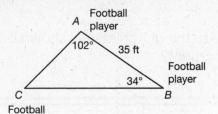

2. *(103)* Find the volume of the frustum of the pyramid shown below.

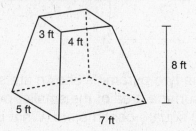

3. *(88)* Solve the strict linear inequality $4x - 3y \geq 3$ for y.

4. *(105)* Evaluate $\begin{bmatrix} 2 & -3 \\ 0 & 1 \\ 4 & 3 \end{bmatrix} \times \begin{bmatrix} 0 & -3 & 4 \\ 2 & 0 & 2 \end{bmatrix}$.

5. *(67)* Identify the type of transformation illustrated below.

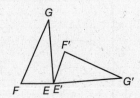

6. *(98)* Find the measure of $\angle C$ in the triangle below. Round your answer to the nearest hundredth of a degree.

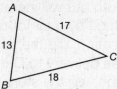

7. *(101)* Determine the value of x in the diagram below.

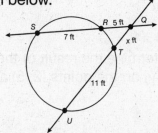

8. *(100)* Write a point matrix for $\overline{EF}$. Add the point matrix to the matrix $\begin{bmatrix} 2 & 2 \\ 2 & 2 \end{bmatrix}$. Graph the line represented by the new matrix.

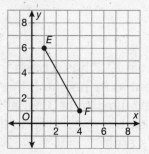

9. *(66)* A regular hexagon has a side length of 48 cm. What is the area of the hexagon?

10. *(104)* Use the figure shown below and the given information to find the measure of each arc.

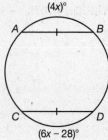

Test 21–continued

11. (95) Carla lives 7 miles north and 7 miles west of a furniture store that offers free delivery for 10 miles in any direction. The store will be moving to a new location 6 miles south but will increase its delivery range by a factor of 1.5. From its original location, did the furniture store provide free delivery to Carla? From its new location, will the store provide free delivery to Carla? Explain.

12. (102) Determine the result of the dilation $D_{4,4}(x, y)$ on the points $(2, 5)$ and $(-3, 1)$.

13. (77) What is the volume of a right cone with a radius of 7 and a height of 13?

14. (96) Triangle XYZ has a base that is congruent to its height. If the base is dilated by a factor of 3, what is the ratio of the new triangle's area to the original triangle's area?

15. (86) In ⊙A, chords $\overline{VW}$ and $\overline{XY}$ intersect at Z. Suppose $VZ = 8$, $WZ = n$, $XZ = 6 - n$, and $YZ = 4$. Write and solve an equation for n.

16. (81) Solve the system of equations below algebraically.
$$y = \frac{3}{2}x + 7$$
$$y = -\frac{7}{2}x - 3$$

17. (92) Are the quadrilaterals shown below congruent?

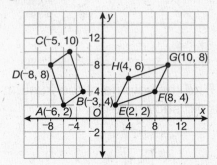

18. (99) The two pyramids shown are similar. The surface area of the smaller pyramid is 120 square centimeters. What is the surface area of the larger pyramid?

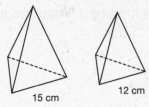

19. (91) Find $\sin\theta$ if $\cos\theta = 0.42$.

20. (97) Write the equations for the concentric circles shown below. Describe how the equations are similar and how they are different.

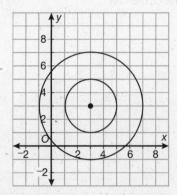

Homeschool Testing Book: Geometry SV 9781600329777

Test 22

1. (96) Naomi is planting a garden in her backyard. Her backyard is a rectangle with a length that is twice as long as its width. Naomi decides that her garden will also be a rectangle, but it will be only two-fifths the length of the backyard and one-fourth as wide. What will be the ratio of the garden's area to the backyard's area?

2. (103) Find the volume of the frustum of the cone shown below.

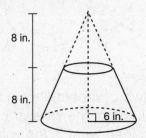

3. (106) Find the perimeter of a regular pentagon that is inscribed in a circle with a radius of 8. Round your answer to the nearest hundredth.

4. (105) The vertices of △DEF are D(−4, 4), E(2, 2), and F(6, 8). Use matrix multiplication to reflect △DEF across the x-axis. Draw the preimage and image in a coordinate plane.

5. (89) The pole for a tent makes a 78° angle with the ground. If the load on the pole is 20 pounds, what are the vertical and horizontal loads?

6. (104) Use the diagram below to prove the first part of Theorem 104-1.
Given: ⊙A, $\overset{\frown}{BC} \cong \overset{\frown}{CD}$
Prove: $\overline{BC} \cong \overline{CD}$

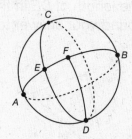

7. (109) In the diagram below, identify a great circle, a segment on the sphere, an angle, and a triangle.

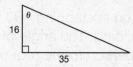

8. (82) In the diagram below, find θ to the nearest tenth of a degree.

```
    θ
16 |
   |_____
      35
```

9. (91) Find cos θ if sin θ = 0.34.

10. (108) The cube shown below has a side length of 1 unit and vertex A at A(0, 0, 0). Identify the coordinates of the other vertices.

Test 22—continued

11. *(110)* A living room is 26 feet long and 19 feet wide. Draw a scale representation of the floor of the living room using a scale of 1 cm : 6 ft. Give your answer to the nearest tenth.

12. *(107)* Rectangle *EFGH*'s base is *b*, its height is *h*, and it has a perimeter of 36 units. Determine the area of the rectangle for $b = 3$, $b = 6$, $b = 9$, and $b = 12$. Based on these results, what conjecture can you make about maximizing the area of a rectangle with a fixed perimeter?

13. *(94)* Find the length of $\overline{DE}$ in the diagram below. Round your answer to the nearest hundredth.

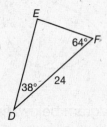

14. *(73)* A person is standing 400 feet away from a building. The angle of elevation from the person to the roof of the building is 58°. Find the height of the building to the nearest foot.

15. *(97)* Find the area of the annulus in the concentric circles shown below.

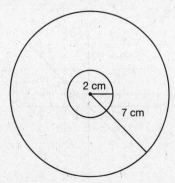

16. *(90)* Reflect the figure below across line *c*, and then reflect the image across line *d*. In the diagram, *c* ∥ *d*.

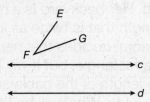

17. *(101)* Determine the value of *x* in the diagram below.

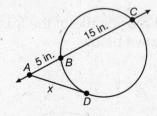

18. *(99)* The two cylinders shown are similar. If the volume of the smaller cylinder is 54 cubic feet, what is the volume of the larger cylinder?

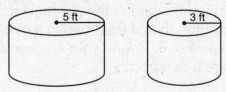

19. *(Inv. 11)* Suppose two numbers, *a* and *b*, are in the golden ratio to each other. If *b* is the smaller number and is equal to 4, what is *a* in simplified radical form?

20. *(102)* Write a point matrix for △*DEF* shown below and use this point matrix to find the coordinates of the image after a dilation with a scale factor of 4.

Test 23

1. (97) A wilderness pilot is dropping food supplies from a small plane and trying to hit the target shown below. The central circle has a 30-foot radius and each annulus beyond that is 10 feet wide. What is the probability that she will hit the shaded portion of the target?

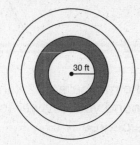

2. (112) Determine the area of the shaded segment of ⊙A in the diagram below. Round your answer to the nearest hundredth.

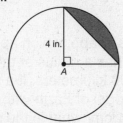

3. (108) Determine the coordinates of two points that are collinear with the points A(9, 6, 5) and B(7, 3, 2).

4. (111) The endpoints of $\overline{ST}$ are S(5, 3, ⁻6) and T(⁻9, 7, ⁻4). Find the midpoint.

5. (103) A traffic cone is partially filled with sand as shown in the diagram below. If the height of the sand in the traffic cone is 9 inches, what volume of sand is in the traffic cone?

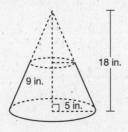

6. (114) Graph the region described by the inequalities $y < x - 4$ or $y > ⁻x + 2$.

7. (106) A circle of radius 5 has been inscribed in a regular hexagon. Find the perimeter of the regular hexagon to the nearest hundredth.

8. (115) Find the surface area of the solid below. Round your answer to the nearest tenth of a square centimeter.

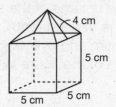

9. (100) The triangle ABC has vertices A(1, 2), B(1, 6), and C(4, 5). △ABC is translated 2 units to the right and 3 units down, resulting in △A'B'C' with vertices A'(3, ⁻1), B'(3, 3), and C'(6, 2). Find the matrix that transforms △ABC to △A'B'C'.

10. (109) Classify triangle QRS shown below according to its angle measures and side lengths.

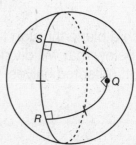

Test 23–continued

11. *(107)* Alan is installing a patio that will contain 324 stone tiles. Each tile measures $\frac{1}{2}$-foot-by-$\frac{1}{2}$-foot. Alan does not know the exact dimensions of the finished patio, but he knows that it is rectangular. What is the minimum perimeter the finished patio could have?

12. *(111)* Find the distance between points $C(4, 7, ^-2)$ and $D(0, ^-1, 5)$.

13. *(115)* Find the volume of the solid shown below to the nearest tenth. Assume that the prism and cylinder are right and that the top of the figure is exactly half of a cylinder.

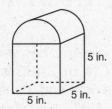

14. *(96)* A rectangle is six times as tall as it is long. If its height is reduced to one-third of its current height, what is the ratio of the new rectangle's perimeter to the original rectangle's perimeter?

15. *(113)* Sketch a plane through the triangular pyramid below that will divide it into two congruent, reflected halves.

16. *(112)* A circle has a radius of 4.4 cm as shown below. Determine the area of a segment formed by a chord with a central angle of 82°.

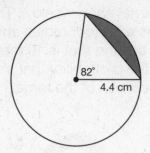

17. *(94)* Find the measure of $\angle X$ in the diagram below. Round your answer to the nearest tenth of a degree.

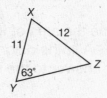

18. *(110)* Earth's shape, which approximates a sphere, has a radius at the equator of about 6400 kilometers. If a student builds a scale model of Earth with a scale of 800 km : 1 cm, what is the radius of the model at its equator?

19. *(114)* Graph the region described by the inequalities $y \le x + 2$ and $y > 2x - 2$.

20. *(113)* Determine whether the solid below has rotational symmetry over the axis shown. If so, give the order of symmetry and the angle of rotational symmetry.

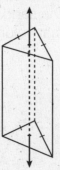

Homeschool Testing Book: Geometry SV 9781600329777

Name _____   Test _____   Score _____

Test Answer Form A

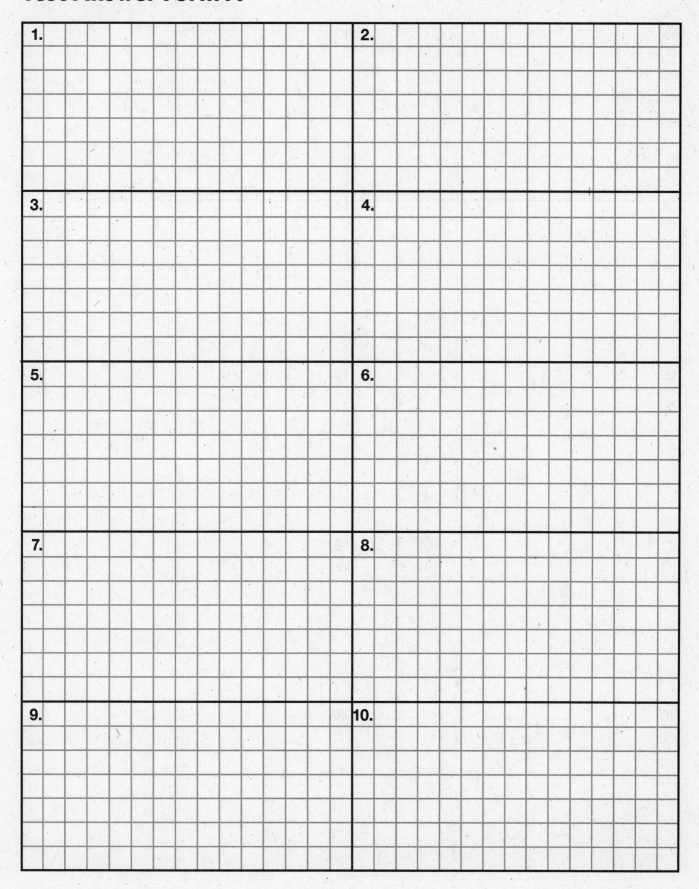

1.

2.

3.

4.

5.

6.

7.

8.

9.

10.

Test Forms
Homeschool Testing Book: Geometry SV 9781600329777

Name _____   Test _____   Score _____

Test Answer Form A–continued

11.	12.

13.	14.

15.	16.

17.	18.

19.	20.

Test Forms
Homeschool Testing Book: Geometry SV 9781600329777

Name _____ Test _____ Score _____

Test Answer Form B

1.	2.
3.	4.
5.	6.
7.	8.
9.	10.

Homeschool Testing Book: Geometry SV 9781600329777

Test Answer Form B—continued

11.	**12.**
13.	**14.**
15.	**16.**
17.	**18.**
19.	**20.**

Homeschool Testing Book: Geometry SV 9781600329777

Name _____   Test _____   Score _____

Test Answer Form C

1.	2.	3.	4.	1.	
				2.	
				3.	
				4.	
5.	6.	7.	8.	5.	
				6.	
				7.	
				8.	
9.	10.	11.	12.	9.	
				10.	
				11.	
				12.	
13.	14.	15.	16.	13.	
				14.	
				15.	
				16.	
17.	18.	19.	20.	17.	
				18.	
				19.	
				20.	

Test Forms
Homeschool Testing Book: Geometry SV 9781600329777

Test Solutions

Test 1

1. The wedge has a measure of 60°; 7 members are in Grade 9.

2. Sample: line a, $\overleftrightarrow{AB}$ or $\overleftrightarrow{BA}$

3. Postulate 8 says that if two points lie on a plane, then the line containing the points lies in the plane. Therefore, since points A and B lie on plane M, then line $\overleftrightarrow{AB}$ lies in plane M.

4. $BD = 4$

5. $YZ = 10$

6. $\overleftrightarrow{UV} \parallel \overleftrightarrow{WX}$

7. Sample: plane BCD or plane Z

8. acute; 20°

9. Points W, X, Y, and Z; $\overleftrightarrow{WX}$ and $\overleftrightarrow{YZ}$; planes M and N

10. 282.5 yards

11. Postulate 6 says that through any three noncollinear points there exists exactly one plane. Since the legs of a three-legged tripod are noncollinear points, they make a single plane. Even if they are uneven, the tripod will be stable and will not wobble.

12. Lines x and y are coplanar; there are no noncoplanar lines.

13. $m\angle WXZ = 77°$; acute

14. $\overleftrightarrow{CG} \parallel \overleftrightarrow{AE}$ and $\overleftrightarrow{BF} \parallel \overleftrightarrow{DH}$

15. Sample:

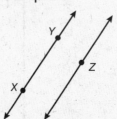

The Parallel Postulate indicates that there is only one line that can be drawn through a point not on $\overleftrightarrow{XY}$ that is parallel to $\overleftrightarrow{XY}$.

16. Sample: Yes, Cesar has applied the Transitive Property of Parallel Lines. He knows that if line C is parallel to the floor and line B is parallel to line C, then line B must be parallel to the floor as well. For line A, since it is parallel to line B, and line B is parallel to the floor, then line A must also be parallel to the floor.

17. Reflexive Property of Congruence

18. Point V

19. The intersection is $\overleftrightarrow{UV}$.

20. $\overrightarrow{AB}$, $\overrightarrow{AC}$, and $\overrightarrow{AD}$

Homeschool Testing Book: Geometry SV 9781600329777

Test Solutions—continued

Test 2

1. $\overleftrightarrow{UV} \perp \overleftrightarrow{ST}$, by Theorem 5-3

2. 32; 102° and 78°

3. Yes. Any two intersecting lines are coplanar.

4. Hypothesis: A prime number is greater than 2. Conclusion: It is odd.

5. Angles 3 and 11, 4 and 10

6. 85 yards

7. 1094; Triple the previous number and subtract 1.

8. 22°; acute angle

9. point

10. m∠1 = 90°; m∠2 = 90°

11. 47.72 square meters

12. complementary: ∠RKM, supplementary: ∠RKL

13. 32

14. 2

15. $15x + 9$

16. $6x + 9$

17. 4.24

18. False. Both numbers can be odd.

19. 60°

20. 3. (*A, B, C*), (*D, E, F*), (*B, E, G*)

Test 3

1. m∠*WXZ* = 83°; acute

2. $x = 55°$, $y = 65°$

3. Lines *s* and *t* are coplanar; there are no noncoplanar lines.

4. Sample:

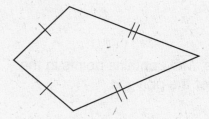

5. 10.7 centimeters

6. The lines are parallel by the Converse of the Alternate Exterior Angles Theorem (Theorem 12-2).

Test Solutions
Homeschool Testing Book: Geometry SV 9781600329777

Test Solutions–continued

7. 64

8. 336 square feet

9. Angle 5 measures 55°, since it is supplementary to an angle that measures 125°. By the Converse of the Alternate Interior Angles Theorem, $m \parallel n$.

10. 5

11. False; $x = {}^-8$

12. 75°

13. (−3.5, 0)

14. 15 inches

15. acute; 15°

16. $C(0.8, 1.5)$

17. Concave. $\overline{MO}$ contains points in the exterior of the polygon.

18. 48.2 centimeters (perimeter), 64 square centimeters (area)

19. Hypothesis: *The product of two integers is divisible by 6.* Conclusion: *One of these integers is divisible by 3, and the other integer is divisible by 2.*

    False. The integers 5 and 6 can be used to contradict this statement.

20. A counterexample is 2 and 2.

Test 4

1. Hypothesis: Lucy buys a salad. Conclusion: Lucy buys a sandwich. Negation of hypothesis: Lucy does not buy a salad. Negation of conclusion: Lucy does not buy a sandwich.

2. Point Y

3. 18 inches

4. There are many adjacent angles in the diagram. Two possible sets are $\angle DCE$ and $\angle ECF$. There are also several linear pairs. One is $\angle DCG$ and $\angle GCH$.

5. 8

6. Angles 1 and 2 both measure 55°, so by the definition of congruent angles $\angle 1 \cong \angle 2$. Since $\angle 1$ and $\angle 2$ are corresponding angles, lines a and b are parallel by Postulate 12.

7. Quadrilateral (rectangle); it is equiangular but not equilateral, so it is irregular.

Test Solutions–continued

8. $m\angle T = 69°$

9. $\overrightarrow{PQ}$, $\overrightarrow{PR}$, and $\overrightarrow{PS}$

10. Perimeter: 30 inches;
    Area: 56.25 square inches

11. 81 squares

12. Hypothesis: $3x - 2 = 7$;
    Conclusion: $x = 3$

13. $QR = 8$

14. $y = \dfrac{1}{2}x - 5$

15. 0

16. Sample:

Hypothesis $x^2 \leq 49$	Conclusion $x \leq 7$	Statement If $x^2 \leq 49$, then $x \leq 7$.
T	T	T
T	F	F
F	T	T
F	F	T

The statement is only false when the hypothesis is true but the conclusion is false. For the statement "If $x^2 \leq 49$, then $x \leq 7$," this is impossible. Therefore, the statement is always true.

17. Triangle ABC is obtuse, because it has one obtuse angle, B.

18. $\overleftrightarrow{AB} \parallel \overleftrightarrow{CD}$

19. 9.3 meters

20. Postulate 8 says that if two points lie on a plane, then the line containing the points lies in the plane. Since points X and Y lie on plane E, then line $\overleftrightarrow{XY}$ lies in plane E.

Test 5

1. Therefore, Joe attended the awards banquet.

2. The circle is $\odot Q$. PR is a diameter. $\overline{PQ}$ and $\overline{QR}$ are both radii. The center of the circle is point Q.

3. Points A, D, and C are collinear. Points A, B, and C are noncollinear.

4. For $n = 1$: $2(1) + 1 = 3$; 3 is prime.
   For $n = 2$: $2(2) + 1 = 5$; 5 is prime.
   For $n = 3$: $2(3) + 1 = 7$; 7 is prime.
   For $n = 4$: $2(4) + 1 = 9$; 9 is not prime.

5. Sample: an acute triangle with angles 60°, 50°, and 70°

6. Sample: Angles 2 and 3 form a linear pair. Therefore, they are supplementary. Using the definition of supplementary angles, since $m\angle 1 = 60°$, then $m\angle 2 = 60°$. Since $m\angle 1 = m\angle 2$, then $\angle 1 \cong \angle 2$. Angles 1 and 2 are alternate interior angles, so by the Converse of the Alternate Interior Angles Theorem, lines a and b are parallel.

Homeschool Testing Book: Geometry SV 9781600329777

Test Solutions–continued

7. m∠FEH = 35°; acute

8. 30 square feet

9. ∠1 and ∠4 are exterior; ∠2 and ∠3 are interior.

10. 30°C

11. 1187.5 feet

12. ∠L corresponds to ∠Q, ∠M corresponds to ∠R, and ∠N corresponds to ∠S. $\overline{LM}$ corresponds to $\overline{QR}$, $\overline{LN}$ corresponds to $\overline{QS}$, and $\overline{MN}$ corresponds to $\overline{RS}$.

13. Hypothesis: Bill has a piano lesson. Conclusion: It is a Monday. Converse: If it is a Monday, then Bill has a piano lesson. The converse is not necessarily true.

14. m∠X = 62°

15. d = 3

16. 112.8 feet

17.
$3(x + 2) = x + 12$	Given
$3x + 6 = x + 12$	Distributive Property
$2x = 6$	Subtraction Property of Equality
$x = 3$	Division Property of Equality

18. The slope is $\frac{1}{2}$.

19. Converse: If $x \le 7$, then $x^2 \le 49$. The original statement is true, but its converse is not true. For example, if $x = {}^-8$, the conclusion is not true.

20. Perimeter: 15 feet; Area: 13.5 square feet

Test 6

1. Therefore, 65 can be divided by 5.

2. 28 square feet

3. Sample: Central angles are ∠RSU and ∠TSU. Minor arcs are $\overset{\frown}{UR}$ and $\overset{\frown}{UT}$. Major arcs are $\overset{\frown}{URT}$ and $\overset{\frown}{UTR}$. Two semicircles are $\overset{\frown}{TUR}$ and $\overset{\frown}{TQR}$.

4. The statement is true.

5. A counterexample is $x = {}^-5$.

6. 45°

7. In these two triangles, E corresponds to Q, F corresponds to R, and G corresponds to S. Therefore, △EFG ≅ △QRS.

8. 12.56 feet

Test Solutions–continued

9.

Statements	Reasons
1. $\angle 1$ is supplementary to $\angle 2$. $\angle 3$ is supplementary to $\angle 2$.	1. Given
2. $m\angle 1 + m\angle 2 = 180°$ $m\angle 3 + m\angle 2 = 180°$	2. Definition of supplementary angles
3. $m\angle 1 + m\angle 2 = m\angle 3 + m\angle 2$	3. Substitution Property
4. $m\angle 1 + m\angle 2 - m\angle 2 = m\angle 3 + m\angle 2 - m\angle 2$	4. Subtraction Property of Equality
5. $m\angle 1 = m\angle 3$	5. Simplify
6. $m\angle 1 \cong m\angle 3$	6. Definition of congruence

10. Transitive Property of Congruence

11. Since every observed peach has a pit, the conjecture is valid based on inductive reasoning. The conjecture can be tested by observing as many peaches as possible. If even one peach is found that does not have a pit, then the conjecture is disproved. The only way to prove this conjecture is to observe every peach. If every peach can be studied, and they all have pits, then the conjecture is true. However, it is impossible to study every peach that exists, so the conjecture cannot be proven.

12. $\overline{GH}$; $\angle F$

13. Hypothesis: *Liz goes to the mountains.* Conclusion: *She goes skiing.* Negation of hypothesis: *Liz does not go to the mountains.* Negation of conclusion: *She does not go skiing.*

14. $\overrightarrow{AB}$, $\overrightarrow{AC}$, and $\overrightarrow{AD}$

15. 17.5 square units

16. 56°

17. Sample: The formula for the area of a rectangle is $A = lw$, so $A = 20$, $l = (2x + 1)$, and $w = 2x$.

$A = 20$	Given
$l = (2x + 1)$	Given
$w = 2x$	Given
$A = lw$	Area formula for a rectangle
$20 = (2x + 1)(2x)$	Substitution Property of Equality
$20 = 4x^2 + 2x$	Distributive Property
$4x^2 + 2x = 20$	Symmetric Property of Equality
$\dfrac{4x^2 + 2x}{2} = \dfrac{20}{2}$	Division Property of Equality
$2x^2 + x = 10$	Simplify
$2x^2 + x - 10 = 10 - 10$	Subtraction Property of Equality
$2x^2 + x - 10 = 0$	Simplify
$(2x + 5)(x - 2) = 0$	Factor

There are two solutions to this factorization, $x = -\dfrac{5}{2}$ and $x = 2$. However, $-\dfrac{5}{2}$ gives a negative length, so it is thrown out. Therefore,

$x - 2 = 0$	Given
$x - 2 + 2 = 0 + 2$	Addition Property of Equality
$x = 2$	Simplify

Substitute $x = 2$ into the expressions for length and width of the rectangle to find the dimensions.

length $= (2x + 1) = (2(2) + 1) = 5$; 5 feet
width $= 2x = 2(2) = 4$; 4 feet

The blanket is 5 feet long and 4 feet wide.

18. $x = 2\sqrt{13}$ meters

Test Solutions
Homeschool Testing Book: Geometry SV 9781600329777

Test Solutions—continued

19. Sample:

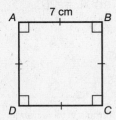

20. 8 inches

Test 7

1. $x = 2.31$; $y = 9$

2. $25°$

3. $XY = 8$; $XZ = 10$; $YZ = 3$

4. $54xy$

5. $(7, 7.5)$

6.

Statements	Reasons
1. $\angle ABD$ and $\angle DBC$ form a linear pair.	1. Given
2. $\overrightarrow{BA}$ and $\overrightarrow{BC}$ are opposite rays.	2. Definition of a linear pair
3. $\overrightarrow{BA}$ and $\overrightarrow{BC}$ form a line.	3. Definition of opposite rays
4. $m\angle ABC = 180°$	4. Definition of a straight angle
5. $m\angle ABD + m\angle DBC = m\angle ABC$	5. Angle Addition Postulate
6. $m\angle ABC + m\angle DBC = 180°$	6. Substitution Property of Equality
7. $\angle ABD$ and $\angle DBC$ are supplementary.	7. Definition of supplementary angles

7. $L = 4\pi$ feet

8. $130°$

9. If it is not a Friday, then Jason does not have a soccer game.

10.

Statements	Reasons
1. $\angle 1$ and $\angle 2$ are supplementary.	1. Given
2. $\angle 2$ and $\angle 3$ are supplementary.	2. Given
3. $m\angle 1 + m\angle 2 = 180°$	3. Definition of supplementary angles
4. $m\angle 2 + m\angle 3 = 180°$	4. Definition of supplementary angles
5. $m\angle 1 + m\angle 2 - m\angle 2 = 180° - m\angle 2$	5. Subtraction Property of Equality
6. $m\angle 2 + m\angle 3 - m\angle 2 = 180° - m\angle 2$	6. Subtraction Property of Equality
7. $m\angle 1 = 180° - m\angle 2$	7. Simplify
8. $m\angle 3 = 180° - m\angle 2$	8. Simplify
9. $m\angle 1 = m\angle 3$	9. Substitution Property of Equality
10. $\angle 1 \cong \angle 3$	10. Definition of congruent angles

11. The formula for the area of a rectangle is $A = lw$, so $A = 48$, $l = (6x - 10)$, and $w = 2x$.

$A = 48$	Given
$l = (6x - 10)$	Given
$w = 2x$	Given
$A = lw$	Area formula for a rectangle
$48 = (6x - 10)(2x)$	Substitution Property of Equality
$48 = 12x^2 - 20x$	Distributive Property
$12x^2 - 20x = 48$	Symmetric Property of Equality
$\dfrac{12x^2 - 20x}{4} = \dfrac{48}{4}$	Division Property of Equality
$3x^2 - 5x = 12$	Simplify
$3x^2 - 5x - 12 = 12 - 12$	Subtraction Property of Equality
$3x^2 - 5x - 12 = 0$	Simplify
$(3x + 4)(x - 3) = 0$	Factor

There are two solutions to this factorization, $x = 3$ and $x = -\frac{4}{3}$. However, $x = -\frac{4}{3}$ gives a negative length, so it is thrown out. Therefore,

$x - 3 = 0$	Given
$x - 3 + 3 = 0 + 3$	Addition Property of Equality
$x = 3$	Simplify

Homeschool Testing Book: Geometry SV 9781600329777

Test Solutions–continued

Substitute $x = 3$ into the expressions for length and width of the rectangle to find the dimensions.

length $= (6x - 10) = 6(3) - 10 = 8$
width $= 2x = 2(3) = 6$

Therefore, the tablecloth is 8 feet long and 6 feet wide.

12. The triangles cannot be proven congruent by the SAS Postulate.

13. Hypothesis: *The product of two numbers is positive.* Conclusion: *Both numbers are positive.* Sample counterexample: $(^-2)(^-3) = 6$

14. $CX = 5$

15. Diagonal $\overline{WY}$ contains points in the exterior of the polygon *WXYZ*. Therefore, polygon *WXYZ* is concave.

16. $x = 52$; the side lengths form the Pythagorean Triple (5, 12, 13) multiplied by 4.

17. 4 square feet

18. 153.86 square inches

19. Therefore, 32 is an even number.

20. $7\sqrt{2}$

Test 8

1. *AB* and m∠*A* (LA); *AB* and m∠*C* (LA); *AC* and m∠*A* (HA); *AB* and *BC* (LL); *AC* and *BC* (HL); *BC* and m∠*A* (LA); *BC* and m∠*C* (LA); *AC* and m∠*C* (HA); *AC* and *AB* (HL)

2. $(^-3, 3)$

3. 201 square inches

4. Parallel

5. $3\sqrt{5}$

6.

Statements	Reasons
1. *WXYZ* is a quadrilateral.	1. Given
2. ∠*W* and ∠*Z* are right angles.	2. Given
3. m∠*W* = 90° and m∠*Z* = 90°	3. Definition of a right angle
4. m∠*W* + m∠*X* + m∠*Y* + m∠*Z* = 360°	4. Formula for the Sum of the Interior Angles of a Polygon
5. 90° + m∠*X* + m∠*Y* + 90° = 360°	5. Subtraction Property of Equality
6. m∠*X* + m∠*Y* + 180° = 360°	6. Simplify
7. m∠*X* + m∠*Y* + 180° − 180° = 360° − 180°	7. Subtraction Property of Equality
8. m∠*X* + m∠*Y* = 180°	8. Simplify
9. ∠*X* and ∠*Y* are supplementary.	9. Definition of supplementary angles

7. ∠*FEG*

8. The triangle is not a right triangle by the Converse of the Pythagorean Theorem.

9. Yes, no, and no

Homeschool Testing Book: Geometry SV 9781600329777

Test Solutions–continued

10. If p, then q: If the zoo is open, then Leo can go to the zoo. AND If q, then r: If Leo can go to the zoo, then Leo can see a zebra. THEN If p, then r: If the zoo is open, then Leo can see a zebra.

11. 64 ft²

12. 71.25 square inches

13. $x^2 \leq 169$ if and only if $x \leq 13$. For the biconditional to be true, both the statement and its converse must be true. In this case, the converse, if $x \leq 13$ then $x^2 \leq 169$, is not true, so the biconditional is not true.

14. $\triangle LMN \cong \triangle FEG$

15. 68°

16. If the measure of an angle is not 90°, then the angle is not a right angle. Both the statement and its inverse are true.

17. $x = 4$

18. $FG = 7.5$

19.

$3(x - 4) = x + 2$	Given
$3x - 12 = x + 2$	Distributive Property
$3x - 12 + 12 = x + 2 + 12$	Addition Property of Equality
$3x = x + 14$	Simplify
$3x - x = x + 14 - x$	Subtraction Property of Equality
$2x = 14$	Simplify
$\dfrac{2x}{2} = \dfrac{14}{2}$	Division Property of Equality
$x = 7$	Simplify

20. $UW > XZ$

Test 9

1. 50.2 inches

2. $y = x + 2$

3. Converse: *If a quadrilateral is a rhombus, then it is a square.* The original statement is true. Its converse is not true.

4. 18 feet

5.
1. F is the midpoint of $\overline{DH}$.	1. Given
2. $\overline{DE} \cong \overline{FH}$	2. Definition of midpoint
3. $\angle EDF \cong \angle FHG$	3. If two parallel lines are cut by a transversal, then alternate interior angles are congruent.
4. $\angle DFE \cong \angle HFG$	4. Vertical angles are congruent.
5. $\triangle EDF \cong \triangle GHF$	5. ASA Congruence Postulate

6. The distance is 2 units.

7. $x = 12, y = 3$

8. $\dfrac{8}{4} = \dfrac{12}{6}$

Homeschool Testing Book: Geometry SV 9781600329777

Test Solutions–continued

9. 108.8 centimeters

10. Scalene; obtuse

11. Sample: The formula for the area of a triangle is $A = \frac{1}{2}bh$, so

$A = 36, b = 3x, h = 2x + 2$	Given
$A = \frac{1}{2}bh$	Area formula for a triangle
$36 = \frac{1}{2}(3x)(2x + 2)$	Substitution Property of Equality
$36 = \frac{1}{2}(6x^2 + 6x)$	Distributive Property
$36 = 3x^2 + 3x$	Distributive Property
$3x^2 + 3x = 36$	Symmetric Property of Equality
$3x^2 + 3x - 36 = 36 - 36$	Subtraction Property of Equality
$3x^2 + 3x - 36 = 0$	Simplify
$3(x + 4)(x - 3) = 0$	Factor

There are two solutions to this factorization, $x = {}^-4$ and $x = 3$. However, $x = {}^-4$ gives a negative solution, so it is thrown out. Therefore,

$x - 3 = 0$	Given
$x - 3 + 3 = 0 + 3$	Addition Property of Equality
$x = 3$	Simplify

Substitute $x = 3$ into the expressions for base and height.

base = $3x = 3(3) = 9$
height = $2x + 2 = 2(3) + 2 = 6 + 2 = 8$

Therefore, the base of the scarf is 9 inches and the height is 8 inches.

12. Sample: (3, 4, 5)

13. Sample: $\triangle ABC$ and $\triangle DEF$ are both right triangles, so the LA Right Triangle Congruence Theorem can be used. The legs $\overline{BC}$ and $\overline{EF}$ are congruent as given. Acute angles $\angle C$ and $\angle F$ are also congruent. Therefore, by the LA Right Triangle Congruence Theorem, $\triangle ABC \cong \triangle DEF$.

14. (3, 2)

15. The tangent is $\overleftrightarrow{VX}$ and the point of tangency is W.

16. 540°

17. 99°, 81°, 99°

18. $\overline{YZ}, \overline{XY}, \overline{XZ}$

19. $\overline{ST}$

20. Sample:

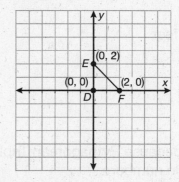

Test Solutions–continued

Test 10

1. $d \approx 1.79$ miles, which is less than 2 miles, so Michael does not live far enough from the school for the bus service.

2. $x = 16\sqrt{2}$

3. $x = 15$; $\overset{\frown}{mAB} = 70°$; $\overset{\frown}{mXY} = 70°$

4. $x = 36$

5. Both lines have a slope of 5, so they are parallel.

6. Suppose that line AB does not contain point C. Assume that line AB and point C cannot be contained by exactly one plane. Since points A, B, and C are noncollinear, this contradicts Postulate 6, which states that through any three noncollinear points there exists exactly one plane. The assumption is contradicted and Theorem 4-2 must be true.

7. 120π square feet

8. $\overline{SU}$; $\angle S$

9. $x = 7.5$; No, because Pythagorean Triples must be whole numbers.

10. First, show that the triangles are similar.

1. $\overline{VW} \parallel \overline{YZ}$	1. Given
2. $m\angle VWX = m\angle YZX$	2. Corresponding angles
3. $m\angle WVX = m\angle ZYX$	3. Corresponding angles
4. $\triangle VWX \sim \triangle YZX$	4. AA Similarity Postulate

$YZ = 6$

Since the triangles are similar, the ratios of the lengths of corresponding sides are equal.

$VW : YZ = WX : ZX$

$\dfrac{VW}{YZ} = \dfrac{WX}{ZX}$; $\dfrac{3}{YZ} = \dfrac{4}{8}$; $4(YZ) = 24$; $YZ = 6$

11. Cylinder

12. $x = 4$

13. $3 < x < 13$

14. Sample:

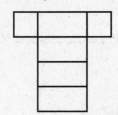

15. $^-1$

Homeschool Testing Book: Geometry SV 9781600329777

Test Solutions–continued

16.

Statements	Reasons
1. $\triangle DEF \sim \triangle JKL$	1. Given
2. $\dfrac{DE}{JK} = \dfrac{EF}{KL} = \dfrac{FD}{LJ} = \dfrac{1}{3}$	2. Given
3. $3DE = JK$	3. Cross multiply
4. $3EF = KL$	4. Cross multiply
5. $3FD = LJ$	5. Cross multiply
6. perimeter of $\triangle JKL = JK + KL + LJ$	6. Definition of perimeter
7. perimeter of $\triangle JKL = 3DE + 3EF + 3FD$	7. Substitute
8. perimeter of $\triangle JKL = 3(DE + EF + FD)$	8. Simplify
9. perimeter of $\triangle DEF = DE + EF + FD$	9. Definition of perimeter
10. perimeter of $\triangle JKL = 3(\text{perimeter of } \triangle DEF)$	10. Substitute

Therefore, the ratio of the perimeter of $\triangle DEF$ to the perimeter of $\triangle JKL$ is 1 : 3.

17. $\angle QSR$

18. Sample:

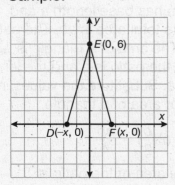

E: (0, 6); D: (^-x, 0); F: (x, 0)

19. 4

20. 14 feet

Test 11

1. 16 feet

2. $m\angle OCA = 90°$

3. 5.5 inches

4. $\angle B$, $\angle A$, $\angle C$

5. Sample:

6.

1. $\dfrac{AC}{DF} = \dfrac{10}{20} = \dfrac{1}{2}$		1. Similarity ratio for $AC : DF$
2. $\dfrac{AB}{DE} = \dfrac{14}{28} = \dfrac{1}{2}$		2. Similarity ratio for $AB : DE$
3. $\dfrac{CB}{FE} = \dfrac{8}{16} = \dfrac{1}{2}$		3. Similarity ratio for $CB : FE$
4. $\triangle ACB \sim \triangle DFE$		4. SSS Similarity Theorem

7. 4π centimeters

8. 4 faces

9. $WZ = 16$; $WX = 20$

10. Assume that $WY \le WX$.
Case 1: If $WY < WX$, then $m\angle Y > m\angle X$, because if one side is longer than another side, then the angle opposite the longer side is larger. This contradicts given information, so WX is not less than WY.

Case 2: If $WY = WX$, then $m\angle X = m\angle Y$ by the Isosceles Triangle Theorem. This contradicts given information, so WY is not equal to WX.

Therefore, $WY > WX$.

Homeschool Testing Book: Geometry SV 9781600329777

Test Solutions–continued

11. 10 inches

12. 3 units

13. $XY = 6.\overline{6}$

14. $x = 26$; $y = 11$

15. By the definition of an isosceles triangle, two of its sides have equal length. To verify that ΔPQR is an isosceles triangle, calculate each of the side lengths.

    $RQ = \sqrt{(1-2)^2 + (3-0)^2} = \sqrt{10} \approx 3.2$

    $PR = \sqrt{(0-1)^2 + (0-3)^2} = \sqrt{10} \approx 3.2$

    $PQ = \sqrt{(0-2)^2 + (0-0)^2} = \sqrt{4} = 2$

    Since $\overline{RQ}$ and $\overline{PR}$ are the same length, ΔPQR is an isosceles triangle.

16. A customer is a museum member *and* gets a discount; true

Statement p	Statement q	Conjunction p and q
T	T	T
T	F	F
F	T	F
F	F	F

    The conjunction is true, because the museum store gives discounts (q is true) to museum members (p is true).

17. $m\angle 1 = 29°$; $m\angle 2 = 90°$; $m\angle 3 = 61°$

18. 1 to 3; 1 : 3; $\frac{1}{3}$

19. 256 square centimeters

20. $13\sqrt{2}$ centimeters

Test 12

1. 6 units

2. $x = 4\sqrt{3}$; $y = 8$

3. $C(1, 3\frac{1}{2})$; $D(\frac{1}{2}, 2)$

4. $m\angle B = 130°$; $m\angle C = 25°$

5. 84 square feet

6. The area of a rectangle is bh. The garden in the diagram has base length a and height b, so its total area is ab. The patio is a triangle. The area of a triangle is $\frac{1}{2}bh$. The height of the patio is $\frac{b}{2}$ and the length of its base is a. Substitute the values into the formula for area of a triangle.

    $$A = \frac{1}{2}h = \frac{1}{2}(a)(\frac{b}{2}) = \frac{ab}{4}$$

    Therefore, the area of the patio is one-fourth the area of the garden.

7. $11\frac{1}{4}$

8. Sample:

Test Solutions
Homeschool Testing Book: Geometry SV 9781600329777

Test Solutions–continued

9. $P = 22$

10. ≈ 10.25 inches

11. 13 feet

12. No, yes, and no

13. 72 square inches

14. 8.5

15. $x = 21; y = 9$

16. Since the two triangles share an angle, we know by the Reflexive Property that $\angle DFE \cong \angle GFH$. It is given in the diagram that $\overline{FG} \cong \overline{FH}$ and $\overline{GD} \cong \overline{HE}$. The ratio of FG to FD can be given by $\frac{FG}{FG + GD}$. By substituting the congruent segments, it can be rewritten as $\frac{FH}{FH + HE}$, which is also the ratio of FH to FE. So the triangles have two proportional sides and one congruent angle. By the SAS Similarity Theorem, they are similar triangles.

17. $x = 12$

18. $m\angle ACB = 65°$

19. Red: 90°; blue: 135°; yellow: 135°

20. $P \approx 17.07$ inches

Test 13

1. $A \approx 1056$ square feet

2. $s = 12.8$ centimeters

3. 47.5 inches

4. $a = 3; b = 10$

5. $m\angle ABC = 115°$

6. To show that $\overleftrightarrow{DG}$ is tangent to $\odot F$, it has to be shown that $\angle DHF$ is a right angle. From the diagram, $\triangle EHF$ is an isosceles triangle, so $\angle FEH \cong \angle FHE$. The acute angles of a right triangle are complementary, so both $\angle FEH$ and $\angle FHE$ are 45° angles. By the Angle Addition Postulate, $m\angle FHE + m\angle DHE = m\angle DHF$. Substituting shows that $m\angle DHF = 45° + 45°$, so $\angle DHF$ is a right angle. Therefore, by Theorem 58-2, $\overleftrightarrow{DG}$ is tangent to $\odot F$.

7. The diagonal $\overline{QS}$ creates $\triangle QRS$ and $\triangle STQ$. Since $\overline{QR} \parallel \overline{TS}$, the alternate interior angles $\angle RQS$ and $\angle TSQ$ are congruent. Segment $\overline{QS}$ is congruent to itself by the Reflexive Property of Congruence. Therefore, $\triangle QRS \cong \triangle STQ$ by the AAS Triangle Congruence Theorem. By CPCTC, $\overline{QR} \cong \overline{TS}$ and $\overline{QT} \cong \overline{RS}$. Since both pairs of opposite sides of $QRST$ are congruent, it is a parallelogram.

8. 84 cubic feet

Homeschool Testing Book: Geometry SV 9781600329777

Test Solutions–continued

9. 54 square feet

10. No, the side measures 14 units and is not congruent to the side that measures 15 units.

11. $100\sqrt{3}$ square inches

12. $y = 2x - 2$

13. 20π square feet

14. $a = 20$; $b = 28$

15. 12 faces

16. $\overline{JK}$ is not parallel to $\overline{FG}$ because $\overline{JK}$ does not divide $\overline{EF}$ and $\overline{EG}$ proportionally.

17. $6\sqrt{5}$

18. Use the Pythagorean Theorem.

    $a^2 + b^2 = c^2$ Pythagorean Theorem

    $5^2 + 8^2 \neq 9^2$ Substitute

    It is not a right triangle by the Converse of the Pythagorean Theorem.

19. If Carlos is hungry, he buys food. The Law of Syllogism is used. The first statement is of the form "If p, then q." The second statement is of the form "If q, then r." The conclusion follows, "If p, then r."

20. $\overline{n}$, $\overline{q}$, $\overline{m}$ with terminal point D, and $\overline{p}$ with terminal point B

Test 14

1. 35 feet

2. $b = 135°$

3. $y = x + 4$

4. $\sin E = \dfrac{4}{5}$; $\cos E = \dfrac{3}{5}$; $\tan E = \dfrac{4}{3}$

5. $AC = 12$

6. Yes, parallelogram $ABCD$ is a rectangle because the diagonals can be shown to have equal length.

7. 552π square centimeters

8. 14 miles

9. $EF = 2DE$; $DE = 2\sqrt{3}$; $EF = 4\sqrt{3}$; $\sin 60° = \dfrac{\sqrt{3}}{2}$, $\cos 60° = \dfrac{1}{2}$, and $\tan 60° = \sqrt{3}$

10. 60 cubic centimeters

11. 72 square feet

12. 144 square meters

Test Solutions
Homeschool Testing Book: Geometry SV 9781600329777

Test Solutions–continued

13. The figure *JKLMN* is reflected across $\overline{JN}$.

14. $A = 5$

15. 10.5

16. 3 units

17. 14 feet

18. 30 inches; kite

19. 62°

20. $|\overline{v}| = 2\sqrt{5}$

Test 15

1. 1099 cubic inches

2. $\angle B = 112°$, $\angle C = 68°$, and $\angle D = 68°$

3. $E'(9, 4)$, $F'(12, 4)$, $G'(12, 7)$, and $H'(9, 7)$

4. $\langle 0, -6 \rangle$

5.

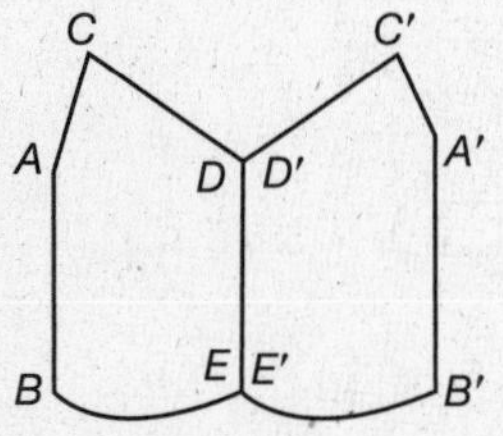

6. $5 + 5\sqrt{3}$ feet

7. $216\sqrt{3}$ square feet

8. 14 feet

9. $\cos 27° = 0.89$

10. $JP = 10$; $KP = 10$

11. $x \approx 76.32$; $y \approx 47.69$; horizontal distance is about 76 feet; height is about 48 feet

12. 149.57 square meters

13. $y = -\dfrac{6}{5}x + 21$

14. 42 cubic feet

15. $(x - 1)^2 + (y - 2)^2 = 4$

16. $P = 24$

17. $P \approx 23.9$ meters

18. $\overline{YZ}$, $\overline{XY}$, $\overline{XZ}$

19. $JL = 10$ inches

Homeschool Testing Book: Geometry SV 9781600329777

Test Solutions–continued

20.

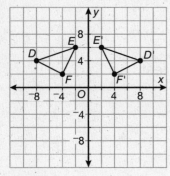

$T : (x, y) \rightarrow (^-x, y)$
$T : D(^-8, 4) \rightarrow D'(8, 4)$
$T : E(^-2, 6) \rightarrow E'(2, 6)$
$T : F(^-4, 2) \rightarrow F'(4, 2)$

Test 16

1. 100 meters

2. About 73 square meters

3.

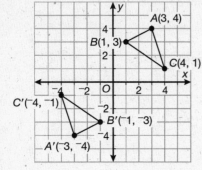

4. Yes; $x = 12$, so the angles are 90°.

5.

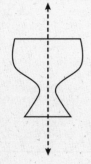

6. $\triangle XYZ$ is rotated clockwise about point Z.

7.

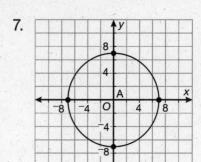

8. $m\angle R = 28°$

9. $\sin 72° = 0.95$

10. $m\angle WXY = 70°$

11. $A = 216\sqrt{3}$ square feet

12. 125.66 square inches

13. $A(^-1, 0) \rightarrow A'(1, 4)$
$B(^-3, ^-3) \rightarrow B'(^-1, 1)$
$C(2, ^-2) \rightarrow C'(4, 2)$

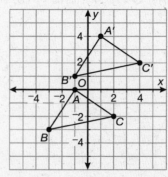

14. 7.15 cubic centimeters

Test Solutions–continued

15. $AB \approx 3.6$, $AD \approx 3.6$, $CB \approx 5.8$, $CD \approx 5.8$

16. $S = 36\pi$ square feet

17. $L = 300\pi$ square inches

18. 28

19.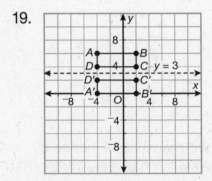

    $A'(^-4, 0)$, $B'(2, 0)$, $C'(2, 2)$,
    and $D'(^-4, 2)$

20. $\langle 15, 6 \rangle$

Test 17

1. Theresa; Theresa is about 238 feet away from the helicopter while Louis is about 140 feet away from the helicopter.

2. $\theta \approx 26°$

3. 60π square inches

4. Yes; 180°; order 2

5. The figure is translated up and right.

6.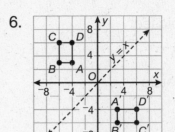

    $A'(3, ^-4)$, $B'(3, ^-6)$, $C'(6, ^-6)$, $D'(6, ^-4)$

7. $(4, 2)$

8. $\tan 25° \approx 0.47$

9. $\vec{a} + \vec{b} = \langle 4, 2 \rangle$

    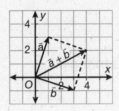

10. $x = 5$; $AC = 37$ feet; $BD = 37$ feet; $DE = 28$ feet

11. $(15, 2)$; $(13, ^-3)$

12.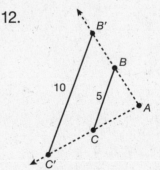

    Since BC was 5 and it was enlarged by a factor of 2, $B'C'$ is 10.

Homeschool Testing Book: Geometry SV 9781600329777

Test Solutions–continued

13. $V \approx 7238.23$ cubic feet

14. $225\sqrt{3}$ square meters

15. $m\angle D = 44°$

16. $PT = 5.4$ feet

17. $(-1, 4)$

18. $x^2 + y^2 = 5$

19. 612 square feet

20. The cross section is a triangle.

Test 18

1. Approximately 3041.38 feet

2. $FX = 8$

3.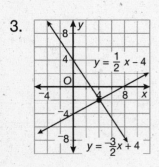

$(4, -2)$

4. No

5. $\theta \approx 42°$

6. $b \approx 10.72$

7. $V \approx 9.8$ cubic inches

8. $x^2 + y^2 = 36$

9. 3; 120°; 360°

10. 96 feet

11. The painting will measure 14 inches by 21 inches; the sketch has a perimeter that is $\frac{4}{7}$ the perimeter of the painting.

12. No, the parallelogram is not a rhombus.

13. $y > -\frac{5}{3}x + \frac{4}{3}$

14. $P = 44.5$ meters

15. The length of $\overline{UV}$ is 16 feet.

16.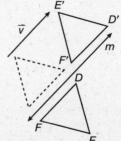

Homeschool Testing Book: Geometry SV 9781600329777

Test Solutions–continued

17. $A'(0, 1)$, $B'(-2, 0)$, and $C'(1, -2)$

18. $x = 87°$

19. $\overline{V}_x = \langle 3, 0 \rangle$, $\overline{V}_y = \langle 0, 5 \rangle$

20. 6π meters or about 18.85 meters

Test 19

1. 23 feet

2. $V \approx 1526.81$ cubic inches;
   $SA \approx 763.41$ square inches

3. $\sin\theta \approx 0.74$

4. $\overline{e} + \overline{f} + \overline{g} = \langle 3, 5 \rangle$

5. Front:

   Top:

   Side:

6. Yes, $QRST$ is a parallelogram.

7.

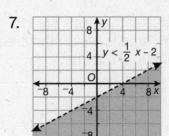

8. $A = 9\sqrt{3}$ square inches

9. $(3, 4)$; $(2, 9)$

10. $AC \approx 14.54$

11. The price of the product is $50 and 30 will sell at this price.

12. $x = 4$

13. $(x + 3)^2 + y^2 = 9$

14. $(x + 2)^2 + (y - 1)^2 = 9$

15.

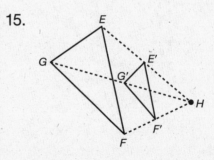

16. $\theta \approx 33.7°$

17. $P = 32$

Test Solutions–continued

18. The ratio of the smaller triangle's area to the larger triangle's area is 9 : 25; the area of the smaller triangle is 108 cm².

19. $\vec{V}_x = \langle 5.56, 0 \rangle$, $\vec{V}_y = \langle 0, 2.25 \rangle$

20. The cross section is a triangle.

Test 20

1. 5 inches by 10 inches; the perimeter of the original photograph negative is $\frac{2}{5}$ the perimeter of the enlarged print.

2. The circles are not concentric. The circles are coplanar, but they intersect at one point, so they cannot have the same center.

3. $TU = 4\frac{1}{2}$

4. $\begin{bmatrix} 1 & 4 \\ 5 & -2 \end{bmatrix}$

5. 180 square feet

6. $m\angle A \approx 50°$

7. $\theta \approx 54°$

8. 3 : 4

9. $\langle 8, 5 \rangle$; the magnitude of the resultant vector is approximately 9.43. The angle from the horizontal is approximately 32.01°.

10. $c \approx 23.0$

11. Jane is approximately $\frac{\sqrt{15}}{4}$ times as far from Rico as she is from the tree.

12. 804.25 square inches

13. $P = 10.4$ inches

14. $x^2 + y^2 = 16$

15. -- --   -- --

16. No solution; the lines are parallel so they share no common points.

17. Yes, *EFGH* is a trapezoid.

18. $m\angle B = 46°$

19. $y > \frac{3}{2}x - \frac{7}{2}$

Homeschool Testing Book: Geometry SV 9781600329777

Test Solutions–continued

20. Front:

Side:

Top:

Test 21

1. The football player at ∠A is approximately 28 feet from the football. The football player at ∠B is approximately 49 feet from the football.

2. $V ≈ 179.98$ cubic feet

3. $y \le \frac{4}{3}x - 1$

4. $\begin{bmatrix} -6 & -6 & 2 \\ 2 & 0 & 2 \\ 6 & -12 & 22 \end{bmatrix}$

5. ΔEFG is rotated about point E.

6. $m∠C ≈ 43.49°$

7. $x = 4$

8. $\begin{bmatrix} 1 & 4 \\ 6 & 1 \end{bmatrix}; \begin{bmatrix} 3 & 6 \\ 8 & 3 \end{bmatrix}$

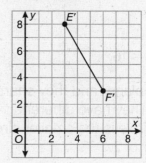

9. $3456\sqrt{3}$ square centimeters

10. $x = 14$; $m\overarc{AB} = 56°$; $m\overarc{CD} = 56°$

11. Yes, Carla lived approximately 9.9 miles from the original furniture store location; yes, the new delivery area is 15 miles in any direction and Carla lives about 14.76 miles from the new location.

12. (8, 20) and (−12, 4)

13. $V ≈ 667.1$ cubic units

14. The ratio of the triangles' areas is 3 : 1.

15. $8n = 4(6 - n)$; $n = 2$

16. (−2, 4)

17. No, ABCD is not congruent to EFGH.

18. 187.5 square centimeters

Test Solutions–continued

19. $\sin\theta \approx 0.91$

20. $(x-3)^2 + (y-3)^2 = 4$
    $(x-3)^2 + (y-3)^2 = 16$

    The circles are coplanar and they share the same center. They have different radii. The larger circle is the smaller circle dilated by a factor of 2.

Test 22

1. The ratio of the garden's area to the backyard's area will be 1 : 10.

2. $V \approx 527.79$ cubic inches

3. $P \approx 47.02$

4. $\begin{bmatrix} 1 & 0 \\ 0 & -1 \end{bmatrix} \times \begin{bmatrix} -4 & 2 & 6 \\ 4 & 2 & 8 \end{bmatrix} = \begin{bmatrix} -4 & 2 & 6 \\ -4 & -2 & -8 \end{bmatrix}$

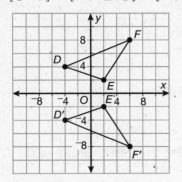

5. The vertical load is about 19.56 pounds. The horizontal load is about 4.16 pounds.

6.

Statements	Reasons
1. $\overset{\frown}{BC} \cong \overset{\frown}{CD}$	1. Given
2. $\angle BAC \cong \angle CAD$	2. Congruent arcs have congruent central angles.
3. $\overline{AB} \cong \overline{AC}, \overline{AD} \cong \overline{AC}$	3. Radii of the same circle are all congruent.
4. $\triangle ABC \cong \triangle ADC$	4. SAS
5. $\overline{BC} \cong \overline{CD}$	5. CPCTC

7. Sample: There are two great circles: great circle AB and great circle CD. A segment on the sphere is $\overline{EF}$. An angle on the sphere is one formed by an intersection of the great circles AB and CD. A triangle is DEF.

8. $\theta \approx 65.4°$

9. $\cos\theta \approx 0.94$

10. $B(1, 0, 0)$; $C(1, 1, 0)$; $D(0, 1, 0)$; $E(0, 0, 1)$; $F(1, 0, 1)$; $G(1, 1, 1)$; $H(0, 1, 1)$

11.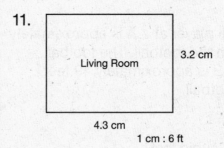

12. For $b = 3$, the area is 45 square units; for $b = 6$, 72 square units; for $b = 9$, 81 square units; and for $b = 12$, 72 square units. Based on these results, the conjecture can be made that for a given perimeter of a rectangle, a square has the greatest area.

13. $DE \approx 22.05$

14. 640 feet

15. The area of the annulus is 45π square centimeters.

Test Solutions–continued

16.
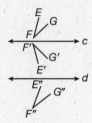

17. $x = 10$

18. The volume of the larger cylinder is 250 cubic feet.

19. $a = 2\sqrt{5} + 2$

20. $\begin{bmatrix} -2 & -3 & 3 \\ 3 & -2 & 1 \end{bmatrix}$;

$4 \times \begin{bmatrix} -2 & -3 & 3 \\ 3 & -2 & 1 \end{bmatrix} = \begin{bmatrix} -8 & -12 & 12 \\ 12 & -8 & 4 \end{bmatrix}$

Test 23

1. $\dfrac{7}{36}$

2. ≈ 4.57 square inches

3. Sample: (13, 12, 11) and (15, 15, 14)

4. The midpoint of $\overline{ST}$ is (−2, 5, −5).

5. 412.3 cubic inches

6.
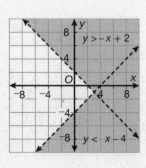

7. $P \approx 34.64$

8. 165 square centimeters

9. $\begin{bmatrix} 2 & 2 & 2 \\ -3 & -3 & -3 \end{bmatrix}$

10. This triangle is equiangular and equilateral, since all side lengths are equal and all angle measures are 90°.

11. 36 feet

12. $CD = \sqrt{129} \approx 11.36$

13. $V = 174.1$ cubic inches

14. The ratio of the new rectangle's perimeter to the original's perimeter is 3 : 7.

15.
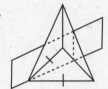

16. ≈ 4.26 square centimeters

17. $m\angle X \approx 62.2°$

18. 8 cm

Homeschool Testing Book: Geometry SV 9781600329777

19.

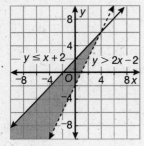

20. Yes; the solid has rotational symmetry and the order of symmetry is 3, and the angle of symmetry is 120°.